LAUNCHING ME, INC.

IT'S TIME TO LEAP FROM THE RUNNING WHEEL AND LIVE YOUR LIFE ON PURPOSE.

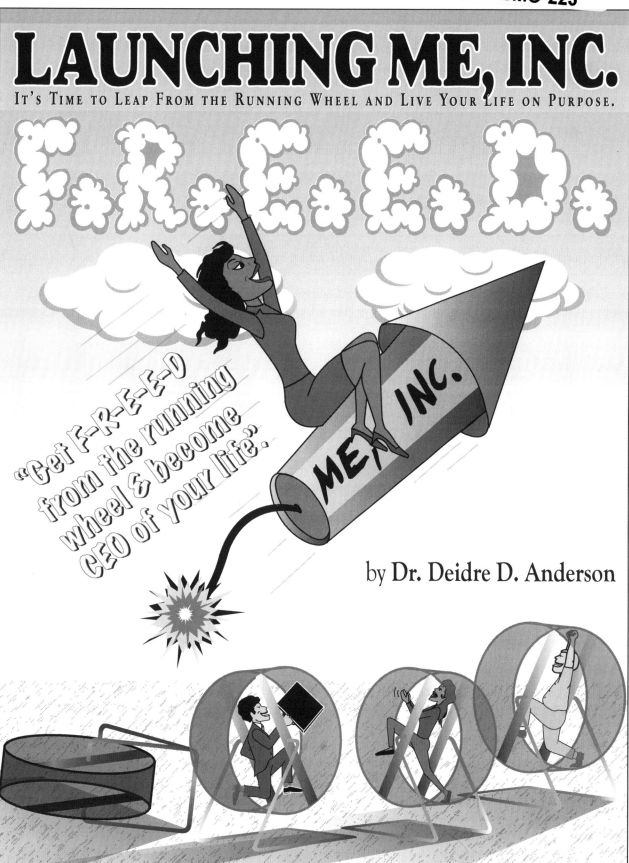

F•R•E•E•D•

"Get F-R-E-E-D from the running wheel & become CEO of your life".

ME, INC.

by Dr. Deidre D. Anderson

Launching Me, Inc.
It's Time to Leap from the Running Wheel
and Live Your Life on Purpose

Dr. Deidre Anderson

ISBN-10 0982790724
ISBN-13 9780982790724

For additional copies, or to contact the author:
    www.trailblazers-inc.com
    www.drdeidreanderson.com
    www.launchingmeinc.com

Edited by Andrea H. Riley.
Front Cover design by Dandridge Designs.

Printed in the United States of America.

LAUNCHING ME, INC.

IT'S TIME TO LEAP FROM THE RUNNING WHEEL AND LIVE YOUR LIFE ON PURPOSE.

F.R.E.E.D.

"Get F-R-E-E-D from the running wheel & become CEO of your life".

ME, INC.

by Dr. Deidre D. Anderson

Table of Contents

Chapter II
Reveal the Truth:

Chapter III
Explore Your Options:

Chapter IV
Establish Goals & Priorities:

Chapter V
Do It!:

Life on the Running Wheel

D o you feel like a hamster on the running wheel of life? Charging full steam ahead? Expending all of your energy, effort and time? Only to look up and find yourself in the same place?

Are you being suffocated by over-commitment? Running from one activity to the next? Gasping for air? With barely a second to catch your breath? Merely to discover that everything you really wanted to accomplish remains untouched?

Is your day spent living from crisis-to-crisis? Working hard to put out fires? Spending countless hours tending to the urgencies of others and doing damage control? Yet you rarely see yourself making inroads where it really matters?

If you are crushed under the weight of endless responsibilities and are feeling frustrated with your lack of progress despite the dizzying pace of your life, you are not alone. In fact, I find that many people who seek my coaching services do so because they are tired of frantically running around in circles with little or nothing to show for their efforts. Unsuccessful in their attempts to balance family, career and personal obligations, they are stuck on life's running wheel fearing there is no way of escape.

Fortunately, as I have witnessed many times, it is possible to break free! You don't have to live your life spinning your wheels. You do have choices! The first decision that you must make in order to step off of the running wheel is to see yourself as the Chief Executive Officer of your own life—the CEO of ME, Inc.

INTRODUCTION

CEO of ME, Inc.

Corporations have CEOs—chief executive officers who are in charge of leading the business. Take a moment to picture your life as a company, a privately-owned business with you at the helm. What do you see? Describe "your company." Is it struggling to get by? Has it hit a plateau? Is it being neglected? Or is it an up-and-coming success story, marked by growth and development and ever-increasing profitability?

If you haven't been looking at your life from this critical standpoint, I challenge you to begin doing so right now. You are the CEO of your life. That means you are ultimately responsible for the level of success that you experience—both personally and professionally. As the CEO, the buck stops with you. You are held accountable for the mission, vision, core values, and branding of "your company." You run the show.

This may be the first time you've thought of yourself as a CEO. Most people fear being in charge. They would rather play it safe and be in a role that doesn't require them to take responsibility for major decisions. That's because, while no one seems to mind reveling in the glory of success, not many are willing to shoulder the blame when results fall short. CEOs don't have the luxury of pointing the finger at others, nor do they have time to wallow in self pity. They are forced to take personal responsibility for their failures, and to do something about them. After all, CEOs are important people. They're leaders, decision makers, and catalysts for change.

Are you ready to take responsibility for your actions and choices so that you can move forward? I encourage you to think of yourself as the chief executive officer in charge of your life. Go ahead. Grab the reins and take control. Get off of the running wheel. Your future depends upon it!

A Change of Address

Sometimes we become so accustomed to our frantic pace and lack of productivity that we resign ourselves to permanent residency on Running Wheel Row. I don't understand why anyone—particularly a CEO—would settle for that kind of life. Running Wheel Row is not in a nice neighborhood. People don't intentionally move there. They come for a visit and never find their way out.

There are four main roads leading into Running Wheel Row. They are:

- Complacency Lane,
- Emergency Landing,
- Limbo Avenue, and
- Procrastinator's Place.

People become permanent residents by carelessly meandering into town via one of those passageways. I have explained each one in the paragraphs that follow. As you read about these pathways, see if you recognize any as a current or former address belonging to you or others that you know.

Complacency Lane

Residents on Complacency Lane have gotten too comfortable. From their vantage point, life is running fairly smoothly. They are pretty much satisfied with their work, their relationships and their lifestyle, so they become content and refuse to venture outside of their comfort zone. They are stuck in status quo. Like a car that sits idling—they stay in one place and burn energy without moving. Occasionally, they may rev up their engines and make a little noise to prove to others that they are still there, but—at the end of the day—they really don't go anywhere. They make excuses and refuse to change. According to them, it's never the right time. In reality, they have hit a plateau. Deep down, they yearn for something more.

Emergency Landing

Then there is the group that seems to live their lives in perpetual crisis – the residents of Emergency Landing. Often, these are folks who were caught off guard with a crisis. A sudden shift occurred and they were thrown off balance – death, divorce, work changes, deteriorating health, aging parents, relationship failures, turmoil in their children's lives, and the list goes on. The wind was knocked out of them. They scrambled to make sense of things. They found themselves needing to stop and regroup. Yet, before they could recover, they were hit with another crisis. Suddenly, what was meant to be a quick layover became a long-term dwelling place. Exhausted, distracted and consumed by their misfortune, they struggle to recuperate and find themselves spinning their wheels. They are hemorrhaging and unsure of what to fix first, so they end up living from crisis to crisis—stifled

INTRODUCTION

in their attempts to move forward. Life has forced them to make an Emergency Landing. Now, they lack the energy, momentum and traction needed to get off of the ground again.

Limbo Avenue

For various reasons, there are times in life when people struggle with uncertainty. Such is the case for those who reside on Limbo Avenue. Doubt has left them feeling powerless and numb, and they don't know which way to turn. Their movements have become stiff, mechanical and robotic. Unclear about what the future holds, they have retreated into an emotional shell and withdrawn from the outside world. They wait for someone or something to awaken them from their comatose state. In the meantime, they are suspended in motion - marking time on Limbo Avenue as they march in place.

Procrastinators' Place

Perhaps the most crowded street on Running Wheel Row is Procrastinators' Place. The people who live here are stuck on the running wheel due to their own lack of direction and failure to plan. Although they are always busy, residents of Procrastinators' Place are constantly putting off the important things in favor of what's urgent. They are quick to make excuses and rationalize that they will get to the important stuff "later." Of course, "later" never comes and criti-

cal tasks are constantly falling through the cracks or being poorly executed. In this community, tenants rarely take time to plan or set goals. They simply live in the moment. Their lives are disorderly and chaotic, but they never stop to do anything about it. In fact, the only thing they ever seem to have time to do is promise that they will handle everything tomorrow.

Purposeful Pathway

Complacency Lane, Emergency Landing, Limbo Avenue, and Procrastinator's Place—four roads leading to the same dangerous destination. Do you recognize any of them? Are you being held captive on Running Wheel Row? If so, what are you waiting for? Fate? Your lucky break? It's time for you to plan your escape.

Life on the running wheel is taking its toll. Spending day-after-day passively spinning your wheels is causing you to lose ground. Your finances are suffering. Your relationships are taking a hit. Time is slipping through your fingers and opportunities are passing you by.

It's time for a change of address. CEOs take initiative. Make a move. Let your running wheel become your launching pad. Assume your rightful place at the helm of your own life. Embrace your role as the CEO of ME, Inc. and prepare to relocate to The Purposeful Pathway where other CEOs reside.

www.drdeidreanderson.com

Applying Business Best Practices

We've already established that you are the CEO of your life. You are the executive responsible for operational oversight of your own well being. This job comes with a lifetime appointment and critical duties.

Now, I encourage you to focus on your number one customer. How are you treating yourself? Would you still have a job if you were evaluated on how well you've managed your life so far?

In my line of work, it is rare to encounter a CEO without a company action plan. Yet, I've met very few people who have a written plan of action for their lives. Many are wandering through life or simply sitting on the sidelines like passive spectators. As with any CEO who has a laissez-faire attitude, those with a hands-off approach to life often find themselves driving "the company" towards destruction. Invariably, their failure to take an active role in managing their own lives leaves them trapped—high-stepping on life's running wheel and going nowhere fast.

Your job is to work on you. You must decide what role you will play in shaping your life and future. Will you assume the position of CEO or act like a minimum wage earner? Good CEOs are visionaries who accept responsibility for their actions. They are pioneers who are willing to take risks, inspire others, and try creative, new things. They don't give up easily or quit when their first attempt doesn't go as planned; they understand that the stakes are high and are willing to go the extra mile and pay the cost to persevere.

The CEO mindset is the same kind of committed approach that is required from you to run your life effectively. If you are going to accept the CEO position, you can't do the minimum and expect to skate by or simply complain, make excuses and "clock out" when things get tough.

I have been a strategic planning consultant and coach for more than a decade. In my work, I guide executives through a systematic process that eventually unfolds into an action plan. It is a painstaking effort that forces organizational leaders to imagine the Ideal Future while grappling with the realities of their current situation so that they can close the gap that separates the two. While a written strategy is the most tangible outcome, I find there is great value in the process itself. The practice of reflection, analysis and debate, along with the resulting commitment to common goals and priorities, is priceless.

Now, my friend, you are positioned to embark upon a similar process. This workbook provides you with the same tools that I use to help organizational leaders achieve their corporate goals.

INTRODUCTION

The only difference is that, instead of creating a strategic plan for an organization, you are going to develop a strategic plan for your life.

When we take time to complete a Strategic Life Plan and discipline ourselves to use it as a guide for our daily decision making, we are freed from the chaos of the running wheel and empowered to live more purposeful, fulfilled lives. Like the people who come to me for help in developing a strategic plan for their organizations, you are responsible for the oversight of a very important entity. You are the CEO of ME, Inc.

My Story

In 2005, my family suffered a devastating tragedy when my nephew was killed in a head-on automobile collision. At the time, I was racing through life on the running wheel—pursuing my doctoral degree, establishing my new business, leading a women's ministry—yet barely having time for what mattered most. My life was full of activities, but some of the most important relationships in my life—including my own self care—were suffering from neglect.

The death of my nephew was a wake-up call for me. I recognized how quickly time can slip through your fingers and how costly it is when you don't spend your life putting first things first. A few weeks after delivering the eulogy at his funeral, I began working on my very first Strategic Life Plan—which became the framework for this book.

A Strategic Life Plan is an overall blueprint for your life. It provides a sense of direction and purpose so that you don't live your life simply wandering from day to day. Much like a choreographer plans and arranges movements into a seamless dance, a Strategic Life Plan provides direction so that you can coordinate the various roles and goals in your life with a sense of wholeness and harmony.

My nephew's death reminded me that leading a meaningful life is about finding balance. It's about making choices that align with what is important to you and harmonizing the different components of your life so that they flow together in a silky-smooth rhythm.

A balanced life gives you the strength and courage to say "no" with grace to requests that are not aligned with your purpose. It offers you equilibrium and steadiness in the various phases of your life, so that, although you may not have perfect balance every day, you have a compass that points you back to what is important.

www.drdeidreanderson.com

Summary

It is possible to live by design rather than default. Assume your rightful place at the helm of your own life. Today could be the day that "your company" begins an incredible turn around. Today could be the day you step off the running wheel and truly start living your life on purpose.

As CEO of your life, you are in charge! You're the boss. So it's up to you. Get started today.

The Launching ME, Inc. strategic life planning workbook is dedicated to the memory of my nephew, Heath Hall.

How to Use This Workbook

This workbook is designed to take you on a journey of self-discovery. There are many different ways to use it successfully. You may go at your own pace and, while I strongly recommend that you complete the chapters in order, you are free to proceed in whatever manner you choose. Ultimately, the goal is to assist you in creating a roadmap that enables you to lead a more balanced, fulfilled life.

Specifically, Launching ME, Inc. will help you to:

- Achieve a better understanding of your life purpose and personal identity.
- Identify your core values and integrate them into your daily life.
- Learn to prioritize and focus your time and energy appropriately.
- Become more balanced in your work and personal life.
- Set clear personal and/or professional goals.
- Stay motivated to follow through and achieve your goals.
- Develop a more positive outlook.

Before getting started, I recommend you review the following sections which explain the framework for the workbook.

F.R.E.E.D.

F.R.E.E.D. Coaching Model

When the time arrived for me to select an area of specialization for my doctoral studies, I jumped at the opportunity to concentrate on leadership coaching. Although I have never been very athletic, my admiration for coaching extends back to the examples that I have observed in sports. Top notch coaches help bring out the best in their players. They study the athletes placed in their care – becoming experts on their strengths and weaknesses and learning about their passions and fears. Skilled strategists, they instill discipline in the players and help their teams to devise a plan of action towards victory.

I spent several years during my studies developing and testing the F.R.E.E.D. Coaching Model for lead-

ers. Subsequently, I have used the model as a step-by-step approach to strategic planning for life and business.

This workbook walks you through the process of developing a Strategic Life Plan using the F.R.E.E.D. Coaching Model as a framework. It is the same strategy that I have used time and time again with my clients. The only difference is that I will not be there to walk you through the model. Instead, I am empowering each of you by putting you in the driver's seat and allowing you to become your own coach. Armed with the F.R.E.E.D Coaching Model, you will be able to catch your breath, think about what needs to be done, and coach yourself right off of the running wheel so that you can successfully launch ME, Inc.!

www.drdeidreanderson.com

Chapter Previews

The five chapters in this workbook correspond with the five steps in the F.R.E.E.D. Coaching Model. They are:

Chapter I: Focus Forward

Any worthwhile strategic planning process begins with envisioning an Ideal Future state. I ask my clients to consider the following questions: What will be your company's claim to fame? When customers and others hear your organization's name, what image do you want it to conjure up? What overriding quality do you want in the front of their minds? In other words, who do you hope to become as a company? You must ask yourself the same questions as the CEO of ME, Inc. What will be your claim to fame? When others hear your name, what image will they see? Who do you hope to become?

All of the activities in Chapter 1 are designed to assist you in completing the first step in the F.R.E.E.D. Coaching Model—Focus Forward. The goal of this chapter is to help you concentrate on where you see yourself as you look into the future. It walks you through developing five critical components of your Strategic Life Plan: a) Core Values, b) Vision, c) Mission, d) Key Roles & Relationships, and e) Personal Brand Promise.

Chapter II: Reveal the Truth

Once you have a clear picture of the future you desire, the next step in the process is to assess your current situation. This is one of the most difficult steps because it requires a long, hard look in the mirror. As the CEO of ME, Inc. you must ask yourself some critical questions, such as: Where am I right now? What are my greatest strengths and weaknesses? What gaps exist between where I desire to be and my current state? Am I living out my core values? Are my mission and vision being fulfilled? What impact am I making?

In order to honestly answer these and other questions about your current reality, you will need to review your past history and gather input from those closest to you. This chapter focuses on Step Two in the F.R.E.E.D. Coaching Model—Reveal the Truth. It invites you to look at your current situation from a variety of different angles and perspectives so that you can discover your "blind spots" and assess the gap between where you are and where you desire to go.

Chapter III: Explore Your Options

The road between where you are standing and your desired destination may seem long and difficult. In Chapter 3, you will have an opportunity to brainstorm solutions for closing the gap.

Using a S.W.O.T. Analysis and other creative tools, you will consider such questions as: What can I do to leverage my strengths? Where do my greatest opportunities and threats lie? How can I overcome my challenges and turn around my weaknesses? In what ways might I create stepping stones and eliminate stumbling blocks to improve my chances of successfully moving forward?

The goal of this chapter is to help you discover as many opportunities as you can imagine to move you toward your desired future. You will address the Third Step in the F.R.E.E.D. Coaching Model—Explore Your Options.

Chapter IV: Establish Goals & Priorities

Chapter 4 focuses upon developing a plan of action. This is where you select the options that best suit you and actually draw a step-by-step map to chart your course forward.

Every organization has a restricted pool of resources. As the CEO of ME, Inc., you must keep in mind that your time, money and energy are limited. What strategies offer you the biggest payoff? Which approach might be easiest to implement? How can you allot your resources so that you maximize the return on your investment?

In Chapter 4, you will break your long-term goals into tangible action steps that can be taken each day to move you towards your Ideal Future. You will work to align your daily to do list with your vision, mission and core values. In short, you will Establish Goals and Priorities—Step Four of the F.R.E.E.D. Coaching Model.

Chapter V: Do It!

While planning is important, implementation is at the heart of making change happen. It is disturbing how many organizations invest blood, sweat and tears in the planning process, only to have their well-intentioned plans sit on a shelf and collect dust.

Plans are simply blueprints. As the CEO of ME, Inc., you are responsible for implementing change based on the strategy laid out in your Strategic Life Plan. The final chapter is geared toward stirring your self-initiative. It is designed to give you a jump start so that you may implement your plan, move forward, and track your progress over time. The goal is to motivate you to take Step Five in the F.R.E.E.D. Coaching Model—Do It!

www.trailblazers-inc.com

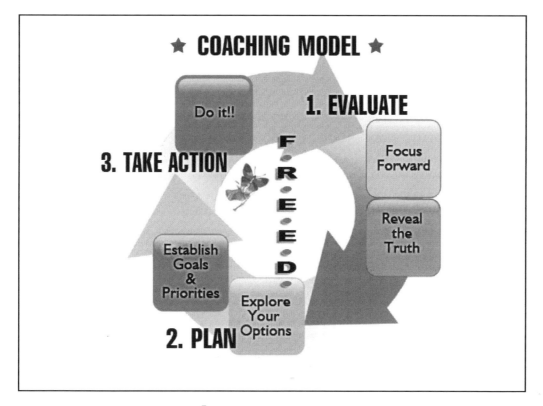

Freeman & Liberty

I recognize that it is often helpful to see examples of what others have written when working through the life planning process. With that in mind, two of my clients have generously agreed to share glimpses of their Strategic Life Plans with you. I strongly recommend that you use their examples as a point of reference rather than copying what they have written word-for-word since each individual's life strategy is unique.

In an effort to protect my clients' privacy, I am simply calling them "Freeman" and "Liberty." A brief description of each one's general background follows so that you can get a sense of who they are and what they want out of life. Whenever I use an excerpt from Freeman or Liberty's Strategic Life Plan, you will see the client's icon next to it.

Freeman

Freeman is a 46-year-old single father with three children, ages 25, 22, and 17. He lives in a large urban city in the northeastern region of the United States and has been employed as a bus driver with the local transit company for 26 years. Freeman has never been married and has primarily raised his children on his own since their mother has been in and out of their lives for the past 16 years. Freeman proudly tells anyone who will listen that his greatest accomplishment is his children. His only daughter, the oldest child, is married now with two children of her own. She lives with her husband and his grandchildren in a neighboring suburb. His oldest son, the middle child, recently graduated from college and is working as an accountant out West. The baby boy will finish high school next year and plans to go into the military.

Facing an empty nest and the prospect of living alone for the first time in more than 25 years, Freeman has been doing some serious soul searching. He recognizes that, for most of his life, he has resided on Emergency Landing. His identity has revolved around sheltering his children from his tumultuous relationship with their mother. He is wondering what he will do with his life now that he no longer has to protect them.

Rumors of forced early retirement for workers with 25+ years of seniority at the transit company also have Freeman rethinking his career options. For many years, he has dreamed of turning his passion for restoring old furniture into a full-fledged business. He is wondering if this may be his window of opportunity to start that business. He decided to write a Strategic Life Plan after attending a career development workshop that was offered through his job.

Liberty

Liberty, a 36-year-old New England native, works as an administrative assistant at a top energy company located in Houston. She took the job as a temporary fix, relocating to Texas after losing her first job out of college to corporate downsizing. Liberty loved everything about the position she landed fresh out of college. She was a human resources coordinator at a public relations firm in Boston; the job was challenging, paid well and afforded her the opportunity to live in close proximity to the small Rhode Island town where she grew up. When she unexpectedly lost her job after eight years due to downsizing, Liberty's ego and financial security suffered a great blow. The situation deteriorated when Liberty, unemployed for nearly three years, was forced to sell her home and move in with her parents.

When a friend encouraged her to apply for the position in Houston, an unenthusiastic Liberty submitted her resume knowing that she was overqualified for the job. Nonetheless, when an offer was extended, Liberty jumped at the chance thinking it might lead to better opportunities. That was three years ago.

Liberty recognizes that she is living on Limbo Avenue. Her esteem and her pocketbook still haven't recovered from the experience in Boston. Although her company offers opportunities for professional development and career advancement, she will need to further her education and go up against some tough competition to receive the promotion she desires. A part of her really wants to take advantage of the tuition reimbursement that the company offers, go back to school and pursue the position. Another part of her is frozen with fear and overcome with insecurities.

A recent event in Liberty's life is nudging her to move forward and boosting her confidence. She accepted a proposal from her boyfriend, Carl, and plans to be married soon. Given this important transition in her life, Liberty has sought the help of a life coach. That's how she learned what a Strategic Life Plan is and decided to write one.

Tips for Using Your Workbook

- **Take time to focus.** Set aside one- to two-hour windows, if possible.

- **Read the introductions and instructions before diving in.** Review the chapter introduction and exercise instructions in your workbook carefully before attempting to complete an exercise.

- **Make copies.** Using the workbook, make copies of each worksheet and Life Plan page before writing on it.

- **Pace yourself.** Go through each workbook exercise at your own pace. You aren't in a race. Take your time.

- **Proceed in sequential order.** I strongly recommend that you complete each workbook exercise in sequential order, as the exercises tend to build upon one another.

- **Fill out your Life Plan pages by hand.** When you are ready, complete your final copy of each Life Plan page neatly in ink by hand; or

- **Use the computer.** Go to our website (www.trailblazers-inc.com), download the appropriate Life Plan page, and complete it on your computer. Save each completed Life Plan page on the computer and/or print it when you are done.

INTRODUCTION

- **Store your completed Life Plan pages.** For those of you who complete your Life Plan pages on the computer, I recommend that you print your pages and purchase a folder or binder that you can use to store your Life Plan pages for easy reference and access.

- **Create your One-Page Life Plan.** Your One-Page Life Plan will serve as a reference for your day-to-day planning. You will be instructed on how to complete your One Page Life Plan in Chapter 4. As with any other Life Plan page, you may complete your One-Page Life Plan by hand or use your computer. Store a completed copy of your One-Page Life Plan in your binder and/or computer, and make another copy for your day-to-day use.

- **Update your plan.** Don't forget to update your goals on a quarterly basis and to review your entire Strategic Life Plan annually (or as needed).

Icons

Icons are used throughout the workbook to identify significant information. Following is a list of workbook icons and their meanings.

Activity
The activity icon indicates an exercise that requires you to complete a specific task or series of tasks.

Checklist
The checklist icon indicates that there is a checklist associated with a particular task or activity. Generally, checklists are included to help ensure that you have completed a task or activity correctly.

Icons, continued

Example from Freeman

The Freeman icon indicates an example from Freeman's Strategic Life Plan.

Example from Liberty

The Liberty icon indicates an example written by Liberty.

Hot Tip

The hot tip icon indicates a practical tip or hint.

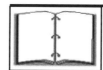

Life Plan Page

The Life Plan page icon signifies that there is a Life Plan page to be completed.

Online Resource

The online resource icon indicates that a copy of the workbook page is available online.

Quote

The "Words to Live By" quote icon indicates an inspirational quote to remember.

Getting Started

The task of creating a Strategic Life Plan seems daunting at first. This self-coaching guide is meant to make the process simple and non-threatening. Feel free to move through it at your own pace and to spend as much time as you need on each exercise.

There are many different ways to use this workbook successfully. Do what feels right to you. Remember: You are the coach. Use the workbook in whatever manner best suits you as long as it helps you move closer to the life you want to achieve.

Take your time. It doesn't matter whether it takes you a month, six months or a year to go through the workbook. If you are serious about getting off of the running wheel, your hard work and effort will pay off.

There is an old Chinese proverb that says, "the journey of a thousand miles begins with one step." Congratulations on taking what could prove to be one of the most significant steps of your life – Launching ME, Inc. Are you ready? Turn the page and let's begin.

Words to Live By

"Don't wait until everything is just right. It will never be perfect. There will always be challenges, obstacles and less than perfect conditions. So what. Get started now. With each step you take, you will grow stronger and stronger, more and more skilled, more and more self-confident, and more and more successful."

- Mark Victor Hansen

FOCUS FORWARD

ENVISION
THE
IDEAL FUTURE

"Dream lofty dreams, and as you dream, so you shall become. Your vision is the promise of what you shall one day be; your ideal is the prophecy of what you shall at last unveil."

\- James Allen

Motivation to Leap from the Running Wheel

My clients kick off the strategic planning process with exercises that challenge them to envision an Ideal Future. I dare them to imagine a time to come when they have escaped the running wheel and the company is functioning at maximum capacity. What does the organization look like, I ask, and what difference is it able to make when they remove all limitations?

The first step in creating your Strategic Life Plan is to Focus Forward. You will dream about a future that is full of possibilities and worth believing in. The goal is that you will see an ideal and unique image of what you can become, a vision so compelling that you will be provoked to fight your way off of the running wheel.

CEOs are change agents. In order to launch ME, Inc., you must be willing to c-h-a-n-g-e. I know that change is not a word most of us want to hear. Mark Twain said the only person who likes change is a wet baby. Psychologists also tell us that until the pain of remaining the same outweighs the pain of change, most of us will simply stay the same. Let's face it. Change is uncomfortable. It forces us to do things differently and to break old habits that bring us a sense of security. Yet, without change, we cannot move forward. If we are ever going to escape the running wheel, we must change.

Change that is successful and sustained over time requires strong motivation. Your vision of ME, Inc. must be compelling enough to convince you to change. Getting off of the running wheel – leaving behind what is comfortable – requires you to "launch" out into a future that may seem uncertain at this point. Although life on the running wheel is far from perfect, at least it is familiar. In this chapter, you will create a clearly defined alternative to the running wheel that will provoke you to take a leap of faith. You will describe your Ideal Future, dream big, and imagine a life without limitations!

Your Ideal Future consists of the following five primary components:

1. **Core Values**: Values are the principles, beliefs and attitudes that guide your decisions, actions and behaviors. Your core values define and distinguish who you are as a person – what matters most to you and what you stand for.

2. **Your Mission Statement**: Your mission is the reason you exist. Your mission statement describes who you are, what you do, how you do it, and why you do it.

www.trailblazers-inc.com

3. **Your Vision Statement**: A vision statement is a picture of the future you want to create. It shows where you want to go and describes what it will be like when you get there. It helps set the boundaries for change.

4. **Your Key Roles & Relationships**: Much of our personal fulfillment in life comes through our roles and relationships with other people. Your values, mission and vision must be explored within the context of your key roles and relationships.

5. **Your Personal Brand Promise**: A personal brand promise is a guarantee of what others can expect from you. It is a statement of value about how you want your decisions and actions to impact those within your sphere of influence.

The Ideal Future is different for everyone. What you envision will be as unique as your fingerprint, a tomorrow filled with dreams created exclusively by and for you. As you assemble the pieces of your Ideal Future, you will build a solid foundation for your life. You will design a blueprint that serves as a compass to guide your decision making as the CEO of ME, Inc.

Determining What Matters Most

Effective CEOs examine the tough decisions they are faced with through the lens of their company's values and priorities. For example, Southwest Airlines' founder Herb Kelleher is committed first and foremost to the customer experience and has made a tremendous effort to hire only pleasant, outgoing employees. As a traveler, I look forward to the welcoming smiles of Southwest's flight attendants and have chosen Southwest over its competitors several times simply because of the warm, friendly service. Another great example of a company that takes its core values seriously is Wal-Mart. Since Sam Walton founded the company in 1962, it has been driven by one core value: everyday low prices. Adhering to that simple value, Mr. Walton has built a world-class empire.

What deeply held values do you possess? You cannot successfully launch ME, Inc. without clearly defining your core values first. Values are the principles, standards, or qualities that you consider important, worthwhile and desirable. They are deeply held beliefs about what is good, right, and appropriate. When you act with integrity, your priorities are in line with your beliefs and your values govern the way you behave, communicate and interact with others.

Those without clearly defined values end up drifting in life. Instead of basing

CHAPTER ONE

their decisions on an internal compass, they make choices based on circumstances and social pressures. They end up trying to fulfill others' expectations instead of their own.

As a young adult, I had a poster hanging on my wall that read: "Stand up for what you believe, even if you are standing alone." These words were a constant reminder of two core principles that my family helped instill in me since my childhood.

- **You need to have a clear understanding of what you believe.** I remember my mother telling me that if you don't know what you stand for, you will fall for anything. Having a strong sense of values as a teenager helped me to withstand the peer pressure that consumed many of my friends. As I grow older, my values continue to anchor me when I am faced with tough choices.

- **You need to be willing to stand up for what you believe.** It's easy to cave in and simply follow the crowd when pressures arise, but it takes conviction and a strong sense of values to go against the grain and do what you believe is right. Values-driven people are often rejected, ostracized and ridiculed by the crowd. Yet, I have found that living a life that aligns with your values provides a sense of peace and well-being that is impossible to experience when you compromise your standards.

In order to get off of the running wheel and launch ME, Inc., you must clearly define your values. Living life without clarity is simply exhausting. It leaves you feeling empty and shallow. When you have clearly defined values, life becomes simpler and more fulfilling. Knowing what you value brings a sense of purpose and direction. It makes decision making easier and builds your confidence that you are making the right choices.

The exercises on the following pages will help you to clarify your core values. As you work through the activities, keep in mind that values are not something you "shop" for. If you spend some time quietly reflecting and answering the questions, you will be able to identify them. Your core values may include qualities such as faith, financial security, accomplishment, adventure, family, spirituality, or fun.

Whatever your values might be, this chapter offers help in defining and recording them. Over the years, I have found that there is something about actually writing down your values that makes you more committed to living them. As you quantify what matters most to you, it will help you decide how to invest your time now and in the future. Are you ready to take another step off of the running wheel?

 # Core Values Exercise
Part 1: Discovering Your Values

Step 1:

Examine the list of values that is provided. Go through each row and circle those values that are most important to you. Also, feel free to add any values that are significant to you that are missing from the list. The blanks below the table are for adding these missing values.

Step 2:

Reduce the total list of values to no more than 20 by eliminating those with lower priority. Simply draw a line through those that have lesser importance.

Step 3:

Reduce the 20 down to 10 core values, again by drawing a line through those having lower priority.

Step 4:

Reduce the 10 down to 5-7 core values.

Step 5:

Write the final 5-7 in the space provided.

 *Freeman's 7 most important values:*

1. Love
2. Faith
3. Self-Control
4. Perseverance
5. Selflessness
6. Family
7. Integrity

 CHAPTER ONE

Core Values List

Abundance	Accomplishment	Adaptability	Adoration	Adventure
Appreciation	Approachability	Balance	Being the Best	Boldness
Challenge	Commitment	Compassion	Composure	Confidence
Connection	Consistency	Contribution	Courage	Creativity
Decisiveness	Dependability	Depth	Determination	Devotion
Devoutness	Dignity	Diligence	Directness	Discipline
Discovery	Diversity	Drive	Eagerness	Effectiveness
Encouragement	Endurance	Enthusiasm	Excellence	Exploration
Faith	Family	Financial Independence	Focus	Freedom
Fun	Generosity	Grace	Gratitude	Growth
Harmony	Health	Honesty	Honor	Humility
Humor	Imagination	Impact	Inquisitiveness	Insightfulness
Inspiration	Integrity	Joy	Leadership	Learning
Love	Loyalty	Making a Difference	Open-Mindedness	Optimism
Order	Originality	Passion	Perseverance	Power
Presence	Purity	Refinement	Reflection	Resilience
Resourcefulness	Respect	Reverence	Security	Self-Control
Selflessness	Serenity	Service	Sincerity	Spirituality
Spontaneity	Stability	Strength	Tranquility	Trustworthiness
Uniqueness	Victory	Vision	Wealth	Wisdom

_____ _____ _____ _____ _____

My 5-7 Top Values:

-
-
-
-
-
-
-

Defining Your Values

Living in a manner that is consistent with your values brings a tremendous sense of self-fulfillment. In the last exercise, you identified the 5-7 values that matter most to you. These are called core values.

Your core values are the essence of who you are. They should apply everywhere and all of the time – at home, at work, at school, or even in an airport filled with strangers. They are to be kept in mind as you go about your daily life.

Now that you have identified the five to seven essential values in your life, you are going to define what those values mean to you. Think about how these values influence your life. Who in your life has demonstrated these values? (i.e., a parent, teacher, coach, mentor, hero, etc.) How did they behave?

Review Freeman's example and answer the questions that follow.

Freeman's Responses

Core Value #1: Love

Why is this value important to you?

Growing up in a poor family, I remember that one of my mom's favorite sayings was, "We may not have much money, but we've sure got a lot of love." Momma always followed that statement up with one of her giant bear hugs. Over the years, especially when my finances were lean, I would close my eyes and hear Momma's voice reminding me that love is what matters most.

Behaviors Defining the Value of Love:
- *ability to sacrifice*
- *willingness to protect*
- *capacity to forgive and overlook shortcomings and quirks*

Core Value #2: Faith

Faith is another value that was dear to Momma. Every Sunday, she would attend services at the local storefront church with me and my two younger brothers in tow. Although I haven't attended a Sunday service in many years, I still hold firmly to the spiritual values that Momma instilled in me and have tried my best to pass them along to my children.

Behaviors Defining the Value of Faith:
- *conviction that things will turn out well even when the odds are against you*
- *belief in a power higher than yourself*
- *living with an attitude of peace, prayer and reverence*

Core Value #3: Self-Discipline

Since I was a child, I have valued routines, discipline and order. I would save my coins in a piggy bank until I had enough money to buy something I really wanted and – even when the peer pressure was on – I prided myself on weighing long-term consequences against short-term gain. I think I have come to value self-disciple even more after watching a lack of discipline destroy the lives of many family members and friends—including my children's mother.

Behaviors Defining the Value of Self Discipline:
- *delayed gratification*
- *self restraint*
- *calmness under pressure*

Core Value #4: Perseverance

I admire those with determination and steadfastness. I've noticed that I find myself constantly rooting for the underdog, perhaps because much of my life has been an uphill battle.

Behaviors Defining the Value of Perseverance:
- *unrelenting courage*
- *an ability to bounce back*
- *persistence*

Core Value #5: Selflessness

I genuinely believe that contentment in life is based more on what you give to others than what you get from them. I watched my mother sacrifice her life for us and, then, in turn, I did the same for my children.

Behaviors Defining the Value of Selflessness:
- *willingness to share what you have with others*
- *putting others' welfare in front of your own*
- *generosity*

www.trailblazers-inc.com

Core Value #6: Family

I value family above everything else. I believe a family should provide refuge and safety for its members. Momma always said that, when everyone else turns a cold shoulder, family continues to embrace you with open arms – no matter what you've done.

Behaviors Defining the Value of Family:
- *unconditional love*
- *loyalty*
- *unity and togetherness*

Core Value #7: Integrity

I believe in honor. I have always taught my children to be honest and tell me the truth no matter what. Money comes and goes. Friends do the same. Your honor and integrity are things that no one can take from you.

Behaviors Defining the Value of Integrity:
- *consistency of character*
- *honesty with others*
- *honesty with oneself*

Core Values Exercise
Part 2: Defining Your Values

Core Value #1: _____

Why is this value important to you?

Behaviors Defining the Value:

_____

_____

_____

Core Value #2: _____

Why is this value important to you?

Behaviors Defining the Value:

_____

_____

_____

Core Value #3: _____

Why is this value important to you?

Behaviors Defining the Value:

_____

_____

_____

www.trailblazers-inc.com

Core Value #4: _____

Why is this value important to you?

Behaviors Defining the Value:

_____

_____

_____

Core Value #5: _____

Why is this value important to you?

Behaviors Defining the Value:

_____

_____

_____

Core Value #6: _____

Why is this value important to you?

CHAPTER ONE

Behaviors Defining the Value:

_____

_____

_____

Core Value #7: _____

Why is this value important to you?

Behaviors Defining the Value:

_____

_____

_____

Core Values Exercise Part 3: Selecting the Final Three

Now that you have identified why the values you selected are important and clarified each one according to the associated behaviors, it is time to narrow the list again. Please review your five to seven top core values, your reasons for selecting them and the behaviors associated with each. Then, choose the three values that are the most important to you. List them in the space provided.

Launching ME, Inc.

Freeman's Top Three Values:

1. *Family*
2. *Love*
3. *Perseverance*

My Top Three Values:

1. _____

2. _____

3. _____

Finishing Touches

Before settling on your final three values, complete the checklist that follows.

Core Values Checklist

Yes	No	Core Values Checklist
		Do your core values represent your most deeply held beliefs and assumptions?
		Do your core values reflect the way you desire to live and conduct yourself on a daily basis?
		Do your core values represent principles that you aren't willing to compromise?

If you have answered "yes" to all three questions, congratulations! You have chosen the right core values. If you have answered "no" to one or more questions, review your core values list. Are you certain about all of the values that you selected? Are there other values that are more important to you? Make the necessary adjustments until you feel satisfied with your final list.

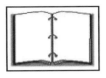 Before moving ahead, take a moment to complete the Core Values Life Plan Page that follows.

 Or, if you prefer, visit our website at *www.trailblazers-inc.com* and download the Core Values Life Plan Page there.

 Put your core values on an index card, laminate the card, and carry it around with you. The next time you are faced with a tough decision, pull the card out and refer to it. Ask yourself which choice best aligns with your core values.

A Ripple Effect

Clearly identifying and understanding your personal core values will energize and affect all areas of your new life as a CEO. In addition to providing a baseline for decision making and problem solving as you move ahead, understanding your core values will help propel you forward in the right direction. Aligning your life with your core values helps provide a sense of fulfillment, well-being and satisfaction. With well-articulated core values in place, you are ready to tackle the next assignment – writing a mission statement for your life.

Words to Live By

"Your beliefs become your thoughts. Your thoughts become your words. Your words become your actions. Your actions become your habits. Your habits become your values. Your values become your destiny."

- Mahatma Gandhi

My Core Values

You're on a Mission

Defining and understanding your core values is the foundation for creating a Strategic Life Plan. Now that you have identified your core values, you are ready to proceed to the next step. It's time to write a mission statement.

Are you on a mission? If I were to ask you, "Who are you and what are you doing here?" would you be able to answer without hesitating, mumbling or being vague? A good CEO is able to answer that question effortlessly. If you don't have an answer – if you don't have a mission statement – you can create one. And, if you do have a mission statement, now is a good time to revisit it.

In my work as a consultant, I have helped dozens of companies compose mission statements. Organizations use mission statements to let people know what they are all about and why they exist. Yet, while many companies proudly display their corporate mission statements on their walls, it is rare to find individuals who actually take time to create a personal mission statement for their lives. Much like a corporate mission statement, your personal mission statement defines who you are, what you're all about, and why you're on this earth. A mission statement allows you to measure your progress toward your ideal life and to evaluate your everyday actions so that they are properly aligned with your core values. It serves as a compass, guiding you and keeping you on course. When you are puzzled about which way to go or have lost your way, your mission statement points you back in the right direction.

Writing a mission statement is one of the most meaningful activities I've ever completed. Over the years, my mission statement has helped to remind me that my life has purpose and significance. It has not only served as a compass, it has been a rallying cry to keep me focused and motivated to move forward.

During the next three exercises, you will gather the information that will be used to develop your mission statement.

Reflections from the Front Porch

My family has a history of longevity. My great-grandmother on my mother's side, L.G. Walker, lived until she was 107 years old. My paternal grandfather, Jay Foster, was 103 when he died. I was blessed to be very close to both of them and to experience the benefit of their wisdom.

As my grandparents aged, I would literally sit at their feet, listening to

CHAPTER ONE

them tell stories about their youth and recount the family history. I particularly remember sitting on my grandfather's front porch in Savannah, Georgia, listening as he sat crossed-legged on his favorite chair recalling the "days of old."

Mission Statement Exercise Part 1: Thoughts from the Rocking Chair

In this exercise, you are going to fast forward and picture your life as you desire it to be when you reach my grandparents' age. Imagine that you are now 95 years old, sitting on a rocking chair outside on your porch. The sun is warm and you can feel the spring breeze gently brushing against your face. You are fulfilled and happy, surrounded by the important people in your life. You look around and smile, feeling pleased with the wonderful life you've been blessed with. Take a minute to visualize the details. Who is there? What do they say? What would your lifetime achievements be? Looking back at your life and all that you've achieved and acquired, all the relationships you've developed – what matters most to you? Write your thoughts in the space provided.

Liberty's Thoughts from the Rocking Chair

I visualize myself on a porch back in Rhode Island, where I plan to retire. My fiancé and I have been married for many years now, and he is sitting beside me holding my hand as we smile fondly at one another. We are reminiscing about how good life has been together.

I refused to allow low self confidence to ruin my life and relationships, so I have long overcome my insecurities. I've lived my latter years with boldness and self assurance. I went back to school and completed my master's degree.

Both my husband and I have had very fulfilling careers and saved enough money so that we could retire comfortably. After retiring, we spent many years traveling and simply enjoying one another's company.

*My Thoughts
from the Rocking Chair:*

Rest in Peace

In the last exercise, you were in your rocking chair. Now, we are going to advance the clock even further. This time, you are going to picture your tombstone. An epitaph is an inscription on a grave-stone written in memory of the one buried there. Epitaphs are like personal mission statements. Those who write them are thinking hard about life and death, and about their own purpose and place in this world.

CHAPTER ONE

Mission Statement Exercise
Part 2: From the Tomb

In this exercise, you will think about the end of your own life. Imagine you are standing in a cemetery looking at your own tombstone. What legacy do you want to leave? Think of the epitaph you would want to see there. Write it in the space provided.

Liberty's Epitaph

Loving Wife; she lived her life with boldness and confidence.

My Epitaph

Paying Tribute

We have proceeded from the rocking chair to the grave. Now, let's consider what will be said by family and friends as they commemorate your life. Imagine your obituary or eulogy. What is it that you want to be remembered for at the end? What did you build? What did you create? For what traits will your friends and family remember and cherish you? What would your lifetime achievements be? What would matter the most at the end of your life?

Mission Statement Exercise
Part 3: The Final Toast

Try to picture what you have achieved by the time of your death. What would you want your family and friends to say as they gave a final toast to you? Take a stab at writing your own eulogy or obituary in the space provided.

Liberty's Obituary

WESTERLY, RI – Liberty (Libby) Harper-Scott, 85, passed away peacefully in her sleep at the home she shared with her husband for more than 40 years.

Libby lived a happy, fulfilled life. She loved to travel with her husband and the two were always on the go, visiting Europe, the Caribbean, Canada, and much of the United States. Libby was always ready for a new adventure, and she especially loved visiting the ocean so that she could walk along the beach holding hands with her husband.

Libby had a long, rewarding career in human resources and was known to be a bold advocate for employees. She won several awards for her dedicated service.

Libby's friends and family will hold a brief memorial service celebrating her life on Tuesday at 10 am at Westerly Town Beach.

My Obituary or Eulogy

CHAPTER ONE

Focus on the Finish Line

The previous exercises have not likely been easy as they forced you to focus on the end of your life. As difficult as the task may have been, keep in mind that it is necessary to focus on the end from the beginning. After all, it will be too late to try to determine the legacy you want to leave while laying on your deathbed. You must consider the legacy you want to leave right now and begin living your life in a way that intentionally begins building that legacy.

Now that you have considered what you want to accomplish during your lifetime, you will actually write your mission statement. A personal mission statement reflects your sense of purpose and meaning in life. It defines who you are and what you want to focus on. It is a tool that can help direct your energy, actions and decisions towards the things you think are most important. Like a roadmap, it helps you stay on course and it redirects you when you have lost your way.

Mission Statement Exercise
Part 4: Putting the Pieces Together

In order to write your mission statement, you will revisit the work that you have done in the previous exercises and bring the key ideas together. First, write down your three core values in the space provided.

Liberty's Top Three Core Values

1. *confidence*
2. *courage*
3. *diligence*

My Core Values

Write your top three core values.

_____

_____

_____

Legacy

Revisit the defining behaviors that you identified for each of your top three values, as well as your thoughts from each of the legacy exercises (rocking chair, rest in peace, and paying tribute). What impact are you hoping to have on the world? How? Summarize the legacy you hope to leave in the space provided.

Bringing It All Together

There are several ways to write an effective mission statement. If you are comfortable with writing, you can simply combine the answers from the previous two questions to form your mission statement. Or, if you prefer, you can use one of the templates provided to get your creative juices flowing. As you write your personal mission statement, remember to keep it simple, clear and brief. Be sure to state everything in the present tense and keep it positive. Your mission statement should inspire and motivate you!

Templates

My mission is to live each day with [your 3 top values], so that [what living these values will contribute to you and the others you interact with]. I will do this by [list the specific behaviors that correspond to your top values from the core values exercise].

Or... My mission is to treasure more than anything [your 3 top values] because [why these values are important to you]. Each day, I [what you will do to live by these values].

Liberty's Mission Statement

My mission is to treasure more than anything confidence, courage and diligence because these attributes will empower me to live a fulfilling and purposeful life. Each day, I will develop my inner self so that I exude confidence; confront fears by taking courageous steps; and diligently apply myself to each task at hand.

My Mission Statement

Finishing Touches

Mission Statement Checklist

Y	N	When you read your mission statement,
		does it capture your unique identity as an individual?
		does it define your life purpose and principal aim in life?
		does it reflect what is important to you?
		does it inspire and give meaning to what you do?
		is it clear and understandable and brief enough to keep in mind?

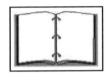 Before moving ahead, take a moment to complete the Mission Statement Life Plan Page that follows.

 Or, if you prefer, visit our website at *www.trailblazers-inc. com* and download the Mission Statement Life Plan Page there.

 Why not follow in the footsteps of leading corporations and display your mission statement for the world to see? Print it on fine stationery, frame it, and hang it in a place where you and others will see it often. This will not only help keep your mission statement in the forefront of your mind, it will increase your accountability to others.

 # Words to Live By

"Twenty years from now you will be more disappointed by the things that you didn't do than by the ones you did do. So throw off the bowlines. Sail away from the safe harbor. Catch the trade winds in your sails. Explore. Dream. Discover."

- Mark Twain

My Mission Statement

A Snapshot of the Future

By now, you should be feeling some sense of relief from the running wheel. Not only have you taken the time to clarify your core values, you have done the difficult work of crafting a personal mission statement. These activities set you apart from the crowd, but we are hardly finished our quest to develop a blueprint for your life.

Visionary CEOs are leaders who are able to clearly see where they are going before they ever get there. Despite what things may look like at the moment, they possess an unwavering conviction that what they imagine is possible. They plan out and document what they see and frequently revisit it—not only to keep themselves motivated—but also to get others to see what they see. With a clear destination in mind, they keep their thoughts and eyes fixed on the target.

As the CEO of ME, Inc., your next task is to create a vision statement. Vision statements are often confused with mission statements. Although the two serve complementary purposes, they are different.

While a personal mission statement focuses on your life purpose, a vision statement is a snapshot of your Ideal Future at an appointed time. It takes your values and places them into the context of what you want to do with them, where you want to be in life, and how you want to affect those around you by a given date. A well-written vision should stretch expectations and aspirations—forcing you out of your comfort zone.

Choosing a Planning Horizon

A planning horizon is the amount of time an organization will look into the future when it is preparing a strategic plan. Before you write your vision statement, you must select a planning horizon for your Strategic Life Plan—a specific time frame that your plan will cover (remember, your vision statement is a snapshot of a particular time in the future).

The simplest way to select your planning horizon is to choose an end date for your plan. This is called your Milestone Date. You can pick any Milestone Date that you want, as long as it is three to five years from now. Perhaps you want to target a significant birthday, retirement, graduation, or some other big event or achievement. It's up to you, as long as it's within that three- to five-year window!

Vision Statement Exercise
Part 1: Choosing a Milestone Date

Freeman's Milestone Date: *June 25, 2015*

Reason(s) for Selecting This Particular Milestone Date:
I chose my 50th birthday.

Record the Milestone Date for your Strategic Life Plan in the space provided. Include a few sentences on why you've chosen this particular date.

My Milestone Date: _____

Reason(s) for Selecting This Particular Milestone Date:

Be, Do, Have, Give

There are four primary components of a personal vision statement:

1. **Be** – Who and what do you want to be: a good friend, parent, leader, etc.?

2. **Do** – What do you want to do: write a book, start a business, learn a new hobby, travel the world, go parachuting, etc.?

3. **Have** – What do you want to have: a new house or car, a jet, good health, a happy family, a strong spiritual life, etc.?

4. **Give** – What do you want to give: share some sort of talent or knowledge with the world, donate money to a worthy cause, pass some values or perspectives along to others, etc.?

www.trailblazers-inc.com

Vision Statement Exercise
Part 2: Thoughts of the Future

Use the boxes provided to write out words and phrases that come to mind for how you envision yourself on your Milestone Date.

Freeman's Vision

Who am I?	**What am I doing?**
• a wonderful father and grandfather • a loving, loyal friend • an entrepreneur • a companion or spouse • an active, contributing community member	• spending lots of time with my grandchildren • growing my upholstery business • building a relationship with that someone special • volunteering at the local recreation center
What do I have?	**What am I giving?**
• a strong, happy family • a mortgage-free home • a tuition account for my grandchildren • a companion or spouse in my life	• my time as a mentor • unconditional love and quality time to my family • excellent service to my customers

My Vision

Who am I?	What am I doing?
What do I have?	**What am I giving?**

Reviewing what you have written so far, draft your vision statement by filling in the blanks provided. Make sure your sentences are: 1) infused with emotion (How are you feeling? What are you sensing?), 2) in present tense (i.e., I am...).

Vision Statement Exercise
Part 3: Writing the Vision

Freeman's Vision Statement

In 2015, I am 50 years old.

I am...
- *a wonderful father and grandfather,*
- *a loving, loyal friend,*
- *an entrepreneur,*
- *a devoted spouse (or companion), and*
- *an active, contributing member of the coâmmunity.*

I am...
- *spending lots of time with my grandchildren,*
- *growing my upholstery business,*
- *building a relationship with that someone special, and*
- *volunteering at the local recreation center.*

I have...
- *a strong, happy family,*
- *a mortgage-free home,*
- *a tuition account for my grandchildren, and*
- *a loving spouse (or companion) in my life.*

I am giving...
- *my time as a mentor,*
- *unconditional love and quality time to my family and friends, and*
- *excellent service to my customers.*

CHAPTER ONE

My Vision Statement

Reviewing what you have written so far, draft your vision statement by filling in the blanks provided.

In _____ *(put your milestone target date here)*, I am _____ years old.

I am…

_____

_____

_____

*Insert the sentences on who you hope to **be** here.*

I am…

_____

_____

_____

*Insert the sentences on what you hope to **do** here.*

I have…

_____

_____

_____

*Insert the sentences on what you hope to **have** here.*

I am giving…

_____

_____

_____

*Insert the sentences on what you hope to **give** here.*

Finishing Touches

A vision is a picture of the future you want to create. It shows you where you want to go and what it will be like when you get there. It helps set the boundaries for change. A well-constructed vision is challenging, yet doable. It is connected to your mission and focused on the future.

www.trailblazers-inc.com

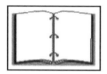

Vision Statement Checklist:

Review your vision statement using the checklist that follows and tweak it accordingly.

Yes	No	Does your vision statement…
		motivate and inspire you?
		stretch and propel you towards greatness?
		align with your mission and core values?
		paint a clear picture of the future you desire?
		use words that drive you to action?

Before moving ahead, take a moment to complete the Vision Statement Life Plan Page provided.

Or, if you prefer, visit our website at *www.trailblazers-inc.com* and download the Vision Statement Life Plan Page there.

Take your Vision Statement a step further by creating a Vision Board. A Vision Board helps you to visually display what your life will look like when your vision statement is lived out. One easy way to create a Vision Board is to cut words and images that represent your vision out of old magazines and newspapers, and then use them to create a collage on poster board. In this digital age, you can also create vision boards to display on your computer screen and mobile devices. Whichever option you choose, your vision board becomes a constant reminder of what you intend to achieve.

Words to Live By

"We are limited, not by our abilities, but by our vision."

–Author Unknown

CHAPTER ONE

My Vision Statement

One Company, Many Divisions

A CEO has to effectively manage all the divisions in his or her corporation. ME, Inc. consists of several interdependent divisions. They include: physical health and wellness; career and professional development; finances and wealth; spiritual well being; friends and family; lifelong learning and personal growth; and recreation and fun. Each of these divisions has many departments and sub-departments that require strategic oversight and management. Similarly, each of us has to direct the numerous and complex domains of our lives. As the CEO for ME, Inc., you must manage each department intentionally and equally well.

In the next exercise, you will write mini-vision statements for the seven departments of ME, Inc. The vision statements for your life divisions will be written in the form of affirmations. An affirmation is a positive statement declaring something to be true. The traditional purpose of affirmations is to create new, empowering beliefs that will override the old, limiting beliefs you may have formed in the past. Affirmations are generally read out loud on a daily basis to help inspire positive thinking and eventually cause your actions to align with those thoughts.

The affirmation statements you write for this exercise describe how you envision each critical area of your life will be when you reach your Milestone Date. Like your vision statement, these statements are written in present tense, as if you are already at that point.

Life Division Affirmations Exercise
Part 1: Critical Success Factors

As a first step, you are going to decide what the three to five critical success factors are for each life division. Success factors are those characteristics or conditions that have a direct and serious impact on your effectiveness in a given area. They serve as measures of performance.

For example, a critical success factor in the health department might be exercise or healthy eating. In the area of relationships, time spent together or creating pleasant memories might be critical success factors. Your critical success factors should align with your core values and beliefs.

Don't worry about adding amounts or percentages to your critical success factors right now (i.e., exercising three times a week, drinking five bottles of water daily or saving 10% of your income). You will work on adding measurements in Step 2. For now, simply record three to five critical success factors for each division of ME, Inc. in the spaces provided.

Selected Examples of Liberty's Critical Success Factors:

Fitness and Health
- walking laps around the local track

Career and Professional Development
- attending management training seminars

Wealth and Finances
- paying off credit cards

Spirituality
- praying consistently

Family and Friends
- visiting parents

Personal Development and Growth
- reading books on self esteem

Recreation and Fun
- weekend trips with my fiancé, Carl

Your Critical Success Factors:

Fitness and Health

■	■
■	■
■	For example, working out at the gym.

Career/Professional

■	■
■	■
■	For example, taking college courses.

Wealth and Finances

■	■
■	■
■	For example, saving for retirement.

Spirituality

■	■
■	■
■	For example, attending church.

Family and Friends

■	■
■	■
■	For example, spending time together.

Personal Development and Growth

▪	▪
▪	▪
▪	For example, reading books.

Recreation and Fun

▪	▪
▪	▪
▪	For example, taking vacations.

Review the critical success factors that you've written for each life division. Do they represent the characteristics or conditions that will most directly affect your success in that particular area? Are you able to use them as measures of success? When you are satisfied with the critical success factors you've selected, move on to the second step in the exercise.

 # Life Division Affirmations Exercise Part 2: Measuring Success

Let's take the second step in writing affirmations for your life divisions. Visualize yourself on your Milestone Date. Think of how you would ideally live your life on a daily basis in each life division. Consider the four principles of "be, do, have, give" as they relate to each area. Using the critical success factors that you have identified, list measurable outcomes, results, and achievements you would like to experience in each key life area. Be specific. For example, in the area of health, you might write: "20 pounds lighter, drinking five bottles of water every day, working out six times a week, eating a nutritious breakfast daily, etc." Try to come up with three to four measurements for each life division. Record your critical success factor measurements in the second column of the table provided on page 66.

CHAPTER ONE

Examples of Liberty's Critical Success Factor Measurements:

Fitness and Health
- *walking 16 laps, 5 days per week*

Career and Professional
- *attending CEU trainings quarterly*

Wealth and Finances
- *paying $250 per month towards additional principal to eliminate credit card debt*

Spirituality
- *praying 30-60 minutes each morning*

Family and Friends
- *visiting parents every other month*

Personal Development and Growth
- *reading one book per month*

Recreation and Fun
- *taking a weekend trip with fiancé every other month*

Life Division Affirmations Exercise Part 3: Writing Affirmations

After you have completed your critical success factors and measurements, try writing a few affirmation sentences for each life area. Remember, affirmations are positive statements that describe you operating at your maximum potential. I generally start mine off with an empowering statement and then list the particulars. So, my health and physical fitness affirmation might read: "I am physically fit and in good health. Every day, I drink five bottles of water and eat a nutritious breakfast. I work out six times a week and weigh 125 pounds." Begin working on affirmations for the areas that you are most passionate about. Then, once you have gotten the hang of it, do the others.

*An Example from
Liberty's Key Life Affirmations*

Wealth and Finances

I am out of debt and financially stable. I pay $250 per month towards additional principle to eliminate credit card debt. I am a saver who contributes no less than 5% of my annual salary towards retirement and puts away at least $50 per month for my vacation fund. I believe in charity and give a minimum of $100 per quarter in donations to further my favorite causes.

CHAPTER ONE

My Affirmations for Strategic Life Areas

Year _____ (milestone date)

Age _____ (age you will be on milestone date)

Strategic Life Area (Key areas of your life)	Critical Success Factor Measurements	Affirmation (What will your life ideally be like in this area by your Milestone Date?)
Fitness and Health		
Career/Professional		
Wealth and Finances		
Spirituality		
Family and Friends		
Personal Development and Growth		
Recreation and Fun		

Finishing Touches

Key Life Area Affirmations Checklist: Review your key life area affirmations using the checklist provided and tweak them accordingly.

Yes	No	Life Affirmations Checklist
		Are they positive and uplifting?
		Do they help create new, empowering beliefs about what you can accomplish in each life division?
		Are the statements clear and concise?

Before moving ahead, take a moment to complete the Key Life Area Life Plan Page provided.

Or, if you prefer, visit our website at www.trailblazers-inc.com and download the Key Life Area Life Plan Page there.

Record yourself reciting your affirmations and burn the recording onto a CD or copy it onto your MP3 player. Listen to your affirmations while exercising, driving in the car, or soaking in the bathtub.

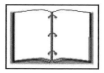

Words to Live By

"If you think you can do a thing or think you can't do a thing, you're right."

–Henry Ford

CHAPTER ONE

My Key Life Area Affirmations

A Brand Called "ME"

You have made valiant strides in your efforts to free yourself forever from the running wheel of life. You have identified your core values and used those core values as a spring board to help you create a personal mission statement, vision statement and affirmations. The foundation for your Strategic Life Plan is nearly complete. Our next step is to focus on identifying your personal brand.

Name the athletic company that comes to mind when you hear the words "Just Do It." What brand of coffee do you think of when you hear the phrase "The Best Part of Waking Up"? Without hesitation, most of us see the Nike swoosh flash before our eyes and smell the aroma of Folgers coffee. That's because both companies have worked very hard to brand themselves using these particular phrases.

Branding is the art of standing out; it is a strategic set of actions that one takes to distinguish or differentiate oneself from the rest of the crowd. In some respect, we deal with branding every day of our lives. CEOs spend millions of dollars trying to convince us that their products are better than those that their competitors sell. Whether the item is laundry deter-

gent, athletic shoes or breakfast cereal, companies work hard to promote their particular brand.

You may be wondering what a brand really is. A brand is that identifiable characteristic that persuades you to use a particular product again and again. It's an image - the mental picture you get when you see a particular logo or hear a familiar jingle. It's also a guarantee that tells you what you can expect from a product today, tomorrow, and into the foreseeable future.

You are a brand. Just like a corporation, you have the ability to create and maintain others' perception of you. While most people see the importance of a company creating and preserving a brand, few recognize that a personal brand is just as important. Much like a corporate brand, your personal brand is your promise of value. It separates you from your peers, your colleagues, and your competitors. A brand deals with how you are perceived in the mind of others. For corporate entities, the audience is their customers. When we look at personal brand, however, the audience is those with whom we have (or want to have) relationships.

Personal branding is about understanding your unique combination of attributes—your strengths, skills, values and passions—and using those attributes to differentiate yourself from others. Your personal brand should set a benchmark for you to strive for in all of your relationships and provide a standard by which others come to know you. As you envision your future, you should imagine yourself intentionally living in a way that validates your personal brand. Ask yourself what you hope to achieve through your personal brand.

Strong brands are distinctive and stand for something unique. They leave a lasting, memorable impression.

Uniquely Me

We all have a personal brand, whether we are aware of it or not. CEOs are intentional about developing and managing their personal brand. They understand that a personal brand is far too critical to leave to chance; they refuse to allow others to simply brand them as they see fit.

The next few exercises will help you to deliberately design and promote your personal brand. The first step in personal brand discovery is listing your unique brand attributes. What makes you distinctive? What makes you notable? What are you passionate about? What are the key characteristics that are clear to anyone who encounters you and how do they add value to others? What are your personal core competencies? Who is the authentic you and how do you express this to the world?

In an effort to help you articulate those attributes, two exercises follow: a self-leadership skills inventory and a communication style profile.

Personal Brand Promise Exercise
Part 1: Self-Leadership Skills Inventory

Self-leadership is the foundation for all leadership and management. If you cannot effectively lead and manage yourself, you will not be able to successfully lead or manage others. After all, you are – first and foremost – the CEO of ME, Inc.

The following inventory is based upon the ABC's of Leadership Competence that I developed to accompany the F.R.E.E.D. coaching model. It addresses seven skills necessary for effective self-leadership. They are:

Agility	**B**alance	**C**haracter	**D**iligence	**E**xcellence	**F**oresight	**G**rowth

What do you have going for you? Read through the following list of self-leadership skills. Put a checkmark next to the two strongest skills that you possess in each category.

Self-Leadership Skills Inventory

Agility

_____ I rise to the challenge, accepting risk and uncertainty.

_____ I recognize when change is necessary to do things better and demonstrate a willingness to confront \ and embrace new perspectives.

_____ I am willing to challenge conventional methods and traditional ways of doing things.

_____ I am open to nontraditional thinking and creative solutions.

_____ I exhibit flexibility and an ability to adjust my behavior and/or approach in response to changes, new information or differences in others' styles or preferences.

_____ I seek alternative approaches and solutions when encountering obstacles.

Balance

_____ I exhibit a willingness to consider diverse perspectives.

_____ I am able to work with and relate to a diverse range of people.

_____ I have a well-rounded perspective.

_____ I keep an open mind.

_____ I am able to orchestrate multiple activities at once to accomplish a goal, focusing on high priority actions and concentrating efforts on the critical few rather than the trivial many.

_____ I maintain a proper balance between my personal and professional life.

Character

_____ I take ownership and accept responsibility for my own decisions, actions and mistakes and the results thereof.

_____ I hold others accountable for shared expectations and am willing to be held accountable as well.

_____ I consistently look at the brighter side of things and maintain a positive attitude, even in the face of adversity.

_____ I demonstrate self-satisfaction, general contentment, and the ability to enjoy life.

_____ My conduct is congruent with my core values and generally accepted moral principles.

_____ I project credibility, poise, and confidence, even under difficult or adversarial conditions.

Diligence

_____ I seek solutions and take action, rather than waiting for others to do so.

_____ I make decisions in a timely manner, regardless of pressure or uncertainty.

_____ I see goals, projects and tasks through to completion.

_____ I do not give up before finishing, even in the face of resistance and challenges.

_____ I bounce back after failures, disappointments and setbacks.

_____ I stay calm and patient, even in high-pressure situations.

Excellence

_____ I refuse to settle for mediocrity or status quo.

_____ I identify the source of my mistakes and determine a course of action to prevent their recurrence.

_____ I make a conscious choice to give of myself to others.

_____ I seek to make a positive impact in others' lives.

_____ I creatively identify, secure and expand resources.

_____ I wisely employ and prioritize the use of resources, including time, money and talent.

Foresight

_____ I exhibit a capacity to think and plan long-term.

_____ I detect potential problems and act before a situation becomes a source of confrontation or crisis.

_____ I strive to develop an integrated perspective that sees patterns and finds connections that others may miss.

_____ I am open and responsive to emerging opportunities.

_____ I have and communicate a clear vision of the future that is manifested in my actions, beliefs, and values.

_____ I look ahead, and don't get stuck in the here and now while attending to a broad range of activities.

Growth

_____ I am aware of my own shortcomings and strengths.

_____ I am dedicated to continuous learning and self-improvement.

_____ I solicit and give honest, diplomatic feedback.

_____ I accept feedback openly and non-defensively.

_____ I create realistic plans that clearly define goals, milestones and results.

_____ I plan in detail how to accomplish large or complex tasks and monitor progress toward that end.

CHAPTER ONE

Based upon the self-leadership skills inventory, list at least five significant attributes you identified about yourself in the space provided.

 *Freeman's Significant Attributes*

- *My conduct is congruent with my core values.*
- *I don't give up before finishing, even in the face of resistance and challenges.*
- *I bounce back after failures, disappointments and setbacks.*
- *I stay calm and patient, even in high-pressure situations.*
- *I take ownership and accept responsibility for my own decisions, actions and mistakes and the results thereof.*
- *I seek to make a positive impact in others' lives.*
- *I exhibit a capacity to think and plan long-term.*

My Significant Attributes

- _____
- _____
- _____
- _____
- _____

www.trailblazers-inc.com

ACTIVITY Personal Brand Promise Exercise Part 2: Communication Style Test

Now that you recognize some of your self-leadership skills, this exercise will help you to determine additional attributes that you possess based upon your communication style. The table that follows contains 16 sets of attributes. Compare the four pairs of attributes in each row. Then, rank them on a scale of 0 to 3, assigning a 3 to the set that best describes you and a 0 to the set that least describes you. When you are done, tally the scores in each column and use the communication style indicator to determine your style.

0= not at all   1= somewhat   2=mostly   3= very much

Communication Style Indicator

IN CHARGE & IN CONTROL		FULL OF ENERGY & ENTHUSIASM		EMPATHETIC & COMPASSIONATE		RELIABLE & STEADY	
PERSISTENT & DETERMINED		SPONTANEOUS & SPUR OF THE MOMENT		THOUGHTFUL & CONSIDERATE		DELIBERATE & DETAILED	
INDEPENDENT & STRONG-WILLED		INSPIRATIONAL & MOTIVATING		NON-DEMANDING & NURTURING		PRACTICAL & ANALYTICAL	
GOAL-ORIENTED & COMPETITIVE		POPULAR & GROUP-ORIENTED		RELATIONAL & LOYAL		ACCURATE & PERFECTIONISTIC	
STRAIGHT-FORWARD & DIRECT		CHARISMATIC & CAPTIVATING		ADAPTABLE & TOLERANT		ORGANIZED & PREPARED	
SELF-SUFFICIENT & FOCUSED		OUTGOING & POPULAR		SUPPORTIVE & TRUSTING		RESERVED & CAUTIOUS	
Total A		Total B		Total C		Total D	

If you scored the highest amount of points in column "A," your dominant communication style is CONTROLLING AND COMMANDING.

If you scored the highest amount of points in column "B," your dominant communication style is CREATIVE AND CONVINCING.

If you scored the highest amount of points in column "C," your dominant communication style is COMPASSIONATE AND COOPERATIVE.

If you scored the highest amount of points in column "D," your dominant communication style is CALM AND CONSCIENTIOUS.

Freeman's Dominant Communication Style

- My *primary style* is a **calm and conscientious** communicator.

- *I also have* **some characteristics** *of a* **compassionate and cooperative** *communicator as well as a* **controlling and commanding** *communicator.*

- *I have* **little or no traits** *of a* **creative and convincing** communicator.

My Dominant Communication Style

Based on the communication style test, complete the following sentences:

My **primary style** is a _____ communicator.
A.   Controlling & Commanding
B.   Creative & Convincing
C.   Compassionate & Cooperative
D.   Calm & Conscientious

I have **some characteristics** of a _____ communicator.
A.   Controlling & Commanding
B.   Creative & Convincing
C.   Compassionate & Cooperative
D.   Calm & Conscientious

I have **little or no** traits of a _____ communicator.
A.   Controlling & Commanding
B.   Creative & Convincing
C.   Compassionate & Cooperative
D.   Calm & Conscientious

www.trailblazers-inc.com

ACTIVITY Personal Brand Promise Exercise Part 3: Additional Attributes

Review the Communication Style at-a-Glance Table below:

Communication Style at-a-Glance Table

People-Oriented and Outgoing

Indirect & Slow-Paced | Direct & Fast-Paced

Compassionate & Cooperative		Creative & Compelling	
Strengths • Good Listener • Understanding • Sincere • Patient • Team Player	**Challenges** • Avoids Conflict and Confrontation • Too "other-oriented" • Feelings easily hurt • Sometimes has the "disease to please"	**Strengths** • Persuasive • Embraces Change • Takes Risks • Confident • Enthusiastic	**Challenges** •Talks too much at times • Impatient • Bored easily • Sometimes lacks detail or follow through
Thrives Best When: There is a "peaceful" environment with little conflict & meaningful relationships.	DIPLOMACY 	**Thrives Best When:** There is a creative environment with opportunities to provide input and be in the spotlight.	DREAMS 
Strengths • Calm •Accurate • Precise • Has High Standards • Analytical	**Challenges** • Slow to change • Perfectionism • Paralysis by analysis • Sometimes overly critical	**Strengths** •Takes initiative •Decisive • Bold • Persistent •Results-oriented	**Challenges** • Pushy • Impatient • Competitive • Sometimes perceived as cold and insensitive
Thrives Best When: There is a slow-paced environment that embraces planning & critical thinking.	DETAILS 	**Thrives Best When:** There is a goal-oriented environment filled with challenges and opportunities.	DRIVE 
Calm & Conscientious		Controlling & Commanding	

Task-Oriented and Reserved

List at least five additional attributes that you discovered about yourself from the Communication Style at-a-Glance Table.

Additional attributes that Freeman discovered about himself from the Communication Style at-a-Glance Table:

- *Calm*
- *High standards*
- *Precise*
- *Sincere*
- *Patient*

Additional attributes that I discovered about myself from the Communication Style at-a-Glance Table:

- _____
- _____
- _____
- _____
- _____

Personal Brand Promise Exercise Part 4: Significant Attributes

Using the findings from your self-leadership inventory and communication style profile, list the 10 strongest personal attributes that reflect your unique style and skills in the space provided. (See the box for additional examples, if you need them.)

Freeman's 10 Attributes:

consistent   responsible
persevering   detail-oriented with high standards
resilient   sincere
calm, cool and collected   patient
long-term thinker and planner   dependable

My 10 Attributes:

_____   _____

_____   _____

_____   _____

_____   _____

_____   _____

Sample List of Attributes

Enthusiastic	Passionate	Inspirational	Practical	Sincere
Funny	Compassionate	Positive	Generous	Encouraging
Open	Warm	Approachable	Knowledgeable	Dynamic
Dependable	Adventurous	Straightforward	Detail-Oriented	Humble

Personal Brand Promise Exercise
Part 5: Emotional Payoff

Your personal brand has an emotional component. Think about your values, mission, vision and other attributes that you have identified. What emotional payoffs do people derive from their relationships with you? What do people gain from being connected with you? Note some of the emotional payoffs and benefits that people get from being in a relationship with you in the space provided.

Emotional Payoffs and Benefits of Being in a Relationship with Freeman

- **Stability** – I don't change up on people. They know what to expect of and from me because I am not easily moved, disturbed or distracted.

- **Peace** – I am a tranquil, calm person. People don't have to be concerned about me stirring up strife, turmoil or disagreements. I am calm, cool and collected even under pressure. My presence helps people feel relaxed; it relieves tension and panic in uncomfortable situations.

- **Confidence** – I follow through and deliver on my promises. People know they can depend on me. If I said I will do it, I will.

- **Solutions** – I am resourceful. People know that, even if I don't have the answer, I will find it. I don't give up easily. I am a solution-oriented problem solver who will persist until the issue has been resolved.

- **Excellence** – I have high standards. I pay attention to detail and people expect that, when I do something, I will do it with excellence. I deliver with quality and distinction.

- **Loyalty** – Once I am in your corner, I generally stay there. I am a trustworthy, dependable and devoted person. People don't have to worry about betrayal, backstabbing or breaches of confidence when it comes to me.

Emotional Payoffs and Benefits of Being in a Relationship with Me:

Personal Brand Promise Exercise
Part 6: Writing My Brand Promise

A Personal Brand Promise is a concise, meaningful, and inspiring statement that sums up the impact a relationship with you will have on someone else. Review your self-leadership strengths, your communications style profile, your list of personal attributes and the information you wrote down about the emotional payoffs and benefits of being in a relationship with you. Combine these thoughts together to create your Personal Brand Promise.

Freeman's Brand Promise

I help people to find solutions, persist, and remain calm in challenging situations. My level-headedness, loyalty and consistency inspire a sense of peace, security and confidence. I have high standards and deliver with quality and distinction every time.

My Brand Promise

CHAPTER ONE

Finishing Touches

Step away for a moment, then come back to review your Personal Brand Promise using the checklist provided.

Personal Brand Promise Checklist

Yes	No	Does your Personal Brand Promise…
		represent what you are willing to deliver to people on a basic level?
		provide a sense of uniqueness and your distinct way of doing things?
		provide people with a sense of the emotional payoff in knowing and having a relationship with you?
		capture how you would want people to describe you after meeting you?

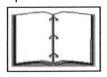

When you are satisfied with your Personal Brand Promise, take a moment to complete the Personal Brand Promise Life Plan Page provided.

Or, if you prefer, visit our website at *www.trailblazers-inc.com* and download the Personal Brand Promise Plan Page there.

Commit your Personal Brand Promise to memory and use it as an elevator pitch. An elevator pitch is a 30-60 second description of who you are and why someone should want to be associated with you. It's an ice breaker and marketing tool – all rolled into one. Traditionally used in business world, the idea is this: "How would you explain your business and make a sale if fate placed you in an elevator with your dream prospect and you only had the time it takes to get from the top of the building to the bottom?" Use your Personal Brand Promise to make a powerful impression of ME, Inc.

Words to Live By

"When I have integrity, my words and deeds match up. I am who I am, no matter where I am or who I am with."
– John Maxwell

My Personal Brand Promise

A Powerful Image

Most brands have a logo. Whether it's a symbol, text, graphic, picture or a mix of these, a logo is one of the most important and distinguishing elements of a brand. Some companies frequently re-brand with a new or updated logo like Pepsi. Others keep their logos more consistent like United Airlines or BMW. For some brands the logo is a representation of the brand essence; for others it is only a small piece of the brand puzzle. Anyway you look at it, people react much stronger to logos than a simple name on a page, especially in this day and age when so much is competing for our attention.

In this exercise, you will design your Personal Brand Logo.

 **ACTIVITY**

Part 7: Personal Brand Promise: Personal Brand Logo Exercise

Your logo will consist of three elements: 1) your name, 2) your photo or a symbol, and 3) your slogan. The first element of your logo is simple. It's **your name**. You can use your first name, nickname, your first and last name, or any combination of your names. The second element is a **photo** of yourself or a symbol of some sort. If you use a symbol, choose one that represents who you are or something that you stand for. You can pick a shape, a letter (or combination of letters), or any type of clip art. It's up to you. Just try to keep it simple. The final element of your logo is a **slogan**. Few people have their own slogan, but almost all companies swear by them. Nike uses "just do it." Apple uses "think different." BMW uses "the ultimate driving machine."

A slogan can get people excited about your personal brand in the same respect. Think about how you want others to connect with you. Think of a catchy phrase to describe other people's experience with you. Perhaps you want to use some of the words from your brand promise. Your slogan can be funny or serious, but it needs to be effective and original to be remembered.

Combine all three elements to create your logo. Sketch it in the space provided or design it on your computer.

Liberty's Logo

My Logo

Finishing Touches

After you have designed your Personal Brand Logo, answer the questions in the checklist.

Logo Checklist

Y	N	When you look at your logo,
		does it catch your eye?
		is it easy to remember?
		is it simple?
		does it represent the essence of who you are and how you want to be regarded?

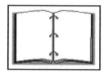

When you are satisfied with your Personal Brand Logo, take a moment to complete the Logo Life Plan Page provided.

Or, if you prefer, visit our website at *www.trailblazers-inc. com* and download the Logo Life Plan Page there.

Take your Logo to the next level of creativity. Play around with different colors, shapes and fonts. Consider drawing unique figures freehand or using clipart. Another option is to pay a professional to create a Personal Brand Logo for you.

Words to Live By

"Self image sets the boundaries of individual accomplishment."

– Maxwell Maltz

CHAPTER ONE

My Logo

Roles and Relationships

As we have done during this entire chapter, we will continue to focus on your Ideal Future. This time, however, we will view that future exclusively through the lens of your key roles and relationships.

What roles do you play? Every task that you address and activity that you pursue is an expression of one or more of your roles. We all have our own list of roles that we play over the course of life, and the list will change over time as new commitments are added and others are completed. Sometimes the role is basic, such as Chef when we make dinner, or more complex, like Spouse or Parent.

Roles and Relationships Exercise
Part 1: Key Roles

You are going to begin by identifying all the key roles that you play in life. Using the list provided, check off the roles that apply to you. Don't forget to include your role as chief executive officer of your life. Also, feel free to add roles that are missing on the lines at the bottom.

Freeman's Key Roles:

- CEO of ME, Inc.
- Sibling
- Parent
- Friend
- Employee
- Neighbor
- Mentor
- Team Member
- Grandparent

My Key Roles:

- ❏ CEO of ME, Inc.
- ❏ Spouse
- ❏ Sibling
- ❏ Son or Daughter
- ❏ Parent
- ❏ Friend
- ❏ Employee
- ❏ Church Member
- ❏ Neighbor
- ❏ Mentor
- ❏ Spiritual Leader
- ❏ Business Person/Owner
- ❏ Team Member
- ❏ Other (list below)
- ❏ _____
- ❏ _____

www.trailblazers-inc.com

Roles and Relationships
Part 2: Relationships

Each of the roles that you play has one or more relationships connected to it. For example, I am a mother with two children. That means that, in my role as a parent, I have two key relationships - one with my son and one with my daughter. Also, I have an older brother and an older sister. Each of these relationships is connected to my role as a sibling.

Revisit the list of roles that you just created. Next to each role, list the primary relationships that are attached to it.

Freeman's Primary Relationships

- *CEO of ME, Inc.*
- *Sibling: Karen, Melvin, Allison, Mary*
- *Parent: Kim, JJ, Kevin*
- *Friend: Chuck, Henry, Fred*
- *Employee: Tim (boss)*
- *Neighbor: Gilda and Ralph, Lennie*
- *Mentor: Ricky*
- *Team Member: Viv, Robert, Sonny (co-workers)*
- *Grandparent: Mark and Kisha*

Roles and Relationships Exercise
Part 3: Relationships to Focus Upon

Select five or six key relationships that you would like to focus upon over your planning horizon. These may be relationships in need of improvement or simply your highest priority relationships. The choice is yours. List those key roles and relationships in the space provided (i.e., parent to Julie, sister to Carol, mentor to Tim, etc.):

CHAPTER ONE

Freeman's List of Roles and Relationships to Focus Upon:

- CEO of ME, Inc.
- Father to Kim
- Father to JJ
- Father to Kevin
- Grandfather to Mark
- Grandfather to Kisha

My List of Roles and Relationships to Focus Upon:

www.trailblazers-inc.com

Words to Live By

"The quality of your life is the quality of your relationships."

- Anthony Robbins

Words from the Heart

I have saved one of the most powerful exercises in this chapter for last. After my nephew died, I recognized even more the significant role that relationships play in having a fulfilled life. In essence, I believe that the quality of your relationships dictates the quality of your life.

You have already identified five or six key relationships that you want to focus upon during your planning horizon. During this exercise, you are going to write letters to yourself from each of those people.

Roles and Relationships Exercise Part 4: Letters from the Future

Find a quiet place where you can concentrate. Imagine that it is 20 or more years from now and you are receiving a separate letter from each of the individuals that you have selected to focus upon. Your job is to write a letter from each individual based upon what you would want the Ideal Future of your relationship with the person to be.

Think of two or three important results you want to accomplish in each relationship you identified. Be specific, touching upon the key things you would want this person to say about you and what you would want your contributions to his or her life to be (build on your personal brand promise). What does your letter say about what the relationship is like at the "present" time (20+ years from now)? What has it been like for them to have you in their lives? What unique contributions have you made that have made their lives better or different? What lessons have they learned from you that they will pass on to others? What is the most important thing you have done in each relationship that has had the greatest impact? Don't be constrained by the resources or conditions of the present. Write about the relationship as you desire it to be.

Freeman's Sample Letter to the Future

A Letter from Kim, My Daughter

Date: June 2031

Dear Dad,

I feel very blessed to have had you in my life all these years. Although we have always been close, and I could talk to you about anything, my appreciation for you has grown by leaps and bounds over the years.

Your unwavering love and commitment to our family has brought stability and peace to my life. You have been an excellent example of how to stand in the face of adversity. This has kept me anchored during the stormy seasons in my life.

Your unconditional love and patience have served as models for my role as parent. I value the principles you instilled in us. Those life's lessons on compassion, loyalty, excellence, self-sacrifice, honesty, integrity, hard work and the importance of family have been a guiding light for all of your children. Your wise words have provided excellent guidance for your grandchildren, as well.

Thank you for being a man of virtue and honor. Thanks for the many selfless years you devoted to raising us. May you live many more years and continue to fulfill your hopes, dreams and desires. I thank God for you.

Love,

Kim

My Letter to the Future

A Letter from _____ , My _____
(individual's name)   *(individual's relationship to you)*

Date: _____
(future date the letter is based upon)

Dear _____ ,
(your name or your relationship to the individual that the letter is from)

Letters from the Future Checklist

Y	N	Have you…
		written the letter from the point of view of your loved one?
		projected far enough into the future (at least 20 years) and written the letter in the present tense?
		described specific characteristics that you would like attributed to your relationship?
		communicated with your heart and not just your head?

If you answered "no" to any of the checklist questions, go back and revise your letter(s) until you can answer "yes" to all of them.

Consider getting your letters custom framed along with a photo of you and your loved one. Display it as a special reminder of what your relationship is becoming or give it to your loved one as a gift.

Words to Live By

"It's a bit too late to start thinking about your legacy when you're on your deathbed, as it is not built in a day, but day by day."

- Daniel Wong

Conclusion

In this chapter, you have worked to define the preferred future for ME, Inc. You've identified your core values, created a mission and vision statement, and developed your brand promise. Congratulations! These are all major steps in targeting your destination so that you can Focus Forward.

Now, it's time for a dose of reality. In the next chapter, you will work to Reveal the Truth about where you currently stand. The goal is not to sap the wind from your sails. The purpose of the chapter is to provide you with an accurate assessment of where you are beginning. Remember, a road map is useless unless we have a concrete starting and ending point. Let's prepare to assess your current location.

Countdown to Launch

Chart your progress by shading in the
steps that you have completed.

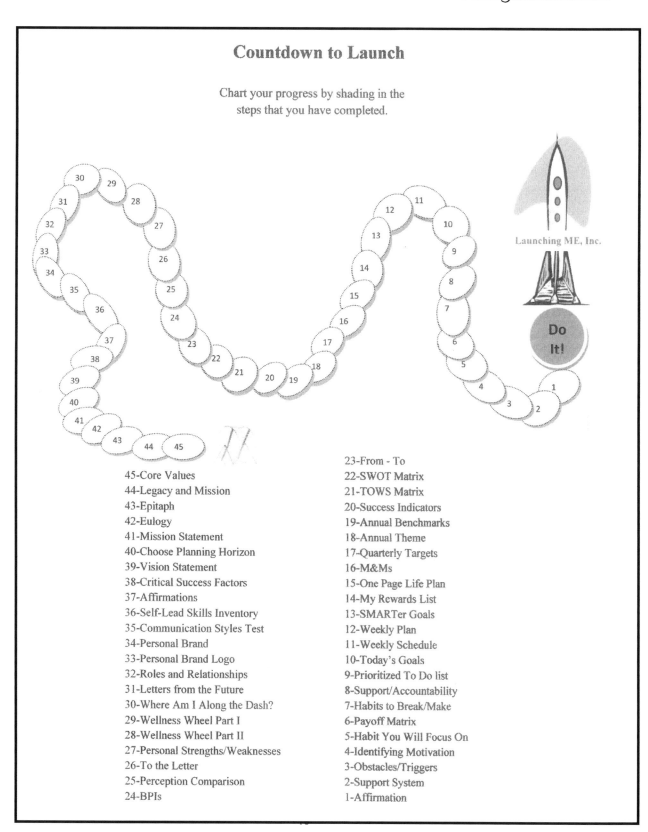

Launching ME, Inc.

Do It!

45-Core Values
44-Legacy and Mission
43-Epitaph
42-Eulogy
41-Mission Statement
40-Choose Planning Horizon
39-Vision Statement
38-Critical Success Factors
37-Affirmations
36-Self-Lead Skills Inventory
35-Communication Styles Test
34-Personal Brand
33-Personal Brand Logo
32-Roles and Relationships
31-Letters from the Future
30-Where Am I Along the Dash?
29-Wellness Wheel Part I
28-Wellness Wheel Part II
27-Personal Strengths/Weaknesses
26-To the Letter
25-Perception Comparison
24-BPIs

23-From - To
22-SWOT Matrix
21-TOWS Matrix
20-Success Indicators
19-Annual Benchmarks
18-Annual Theme
17-Quarterly Targets
16-M&Ms
15-One Page Life Plan
14-My Rewards List
13-SMARTer Goals
12-Weekly Plan
11-Weekly Schedule
10-Today's Goals
9-Prioritized To Do list
8-Support/Accountability
7-Habits to Break/Make
6-Payoff Matrix
5-Habit You Will Focus On
4-Identifying Motivation
3-Obstacles/Triggers
2-Support System
1-Affirmation

CHAPTER 2

REVEAL THE TRUTH

DOING A
REALITY CHECK

"To get where you need to go, you must first know where you are."

— Unknown

www.trailblazers-inc.com

I Have to Start Somewhere

I have a poor sense of direction, so I am quick to grab a map from the rental car counter whenever I am traveling out of town. Somehow, having that piece of paper on the seat next to me makes me feel more secure. I know that I can reach for the map should I get lost while venturing into unknown territory. Yet, I have learned the hard way that simply having a map doesn't do much good if you don't have two critical pieces of information.

Let's say you wanted to head to San Francisco and were using a map to help guide you in your journey. You search the map until you find California and, eventually, San Francisco. You circle your destination using a big red marker. Is your work done? Did discovering San Francisco's location give you all the information you need to plan your trip? Of course not, your destination is just one crucial bit of information that you need. In order to plot your course to San Francisco, you also need to know your current location. Traveling to San Francisco from New York will require a different route than getting to San Francisco from Houston.

In the last chapter, we worked to define the preferred future for ME, Inc. Identifying your values, creating a mission and vision statement, and developing your brand promise are all major steps in targeting your destination. Together, they provide you with your desired end point; however, you are still missing a vital piece of information. You must know where your journey is beginning, as well.

I Am Here

The next step in devising a plan for ME, Inc. is to gain clarity on your starting point. Have you ever noticed the star on a mall directory that notes "you are here"? The purpose of the star is to orient you so that you have a sense of where you are in relationship to where you want to go.

This is critical information: How many times have you hurriedly glanced at a map or directory and rushed off only to find yourself lost or back where you started? Too often, we try to forge ahead without fully considering our current reality. Anxious to move forward, we take off prematurely – unprepared and uninformed – only to end up traveling in circles or hitting a dead end.

It is important that you are strategic in your launch of ME, Inc. You don't have energy or time to waste going around in circles. (You are trying to escape the running wheel, remember?) So before you take off running, let's get a true sense of your current location by doing an honest assessment. This chapter will explore the "R" in the FREED coaching model – REVEAL THE TRUTH. We will examine your readiness to change and look back at some of the ideals you discovered in the last chapter in an attempt to discover the gap between your current reality and your desired future. We will also look at putting measurements in place so that, after you begin your journey, you can determine your progress.

Brace yourself. The truth is never easy to face. This chapter won't be nearly as fun as the last one, but it is critically important to the successful launch of ME, Inc.

Honesty Is, Indeed, the Best Policy

Do you remember the children's classic, *The Emperor's New Clothes*, by Hans Christian Andersen? It is the story of a "CEO" – a self-absorbed, arrogant ruler who is obsessed with his appearance. He is so vain that he purchases an expansive wardrobe so that he can prance around the kingdom showing off his attire. One day, he is approached by two con men pretending to be tailors. The swindlers offer to design an exquisite outfit for the Emperor made out of magical fabric. The cloth, they proclaim, is not only quite beautiful but it also possesses a special power - it is invisible to people who are stupid or unfit for their positions. Enticed by the opportunity to don the latest fashions and sift out the weak, the Emperor falls right into the tricksters' trap and gives them money to make the outfit.

The swindlers' scheme is elaborate. They pretend to call for the finest materials available and then go through the motions of weaving the "invisible" apparel. Concerned about his inability to see his new outfit, the emperor asks his closest advisors to visit so that he can solicit their opinions. With the charlatans hovering nearby to remind them that the outfits are invisible to those who are inept, the men fear being labeled as unwise or unqualified. So, one by one, they lie to the Emperor about the beauty of the clothing that they cannot see.

The Emperor becomes excited! In fact, the compliments of his inner circle bolster his confidence so much that he decides to host a parade the next day to show off his magical outfit. When the Emperor is presented with his "new clothes" in the morning, he and all of his attendants pretend to be impressed by the outfit. They refuse to admit that they cannot see the clothes.

Finally, the Emperor takes his place in the royal procession and begins marching through the streets in his underwear. Too ashamed to admit what they see, the townspeople, who had heard that only losers wouldn't be able to detect the outfit, shout accolades and comment loudly about the beauty of the Emperor's clothes as he strolls past. The ruler, whose ego is being fed by the crowd, marches proudly for hours until he is interrupted by the shouts of a young boy. Puzzled, the child loudly proclaims, "The Emperor is naked!" The boy's candor provokes an outburst of honesty among the crowd which soon confirms the obvious - the ruler is parading around in his birthday suit. Mortified, the Emperor runs quickly back to his castle. While, in the meantime, the thieves flee the kingdom laughing hysterically with his money in hand.

There are some important lessons to learn from the Emperor as you prepare for the launch of ME, Inc. The first lesson is about the critical nature of self-assessment. Accurate self-assessment is based first upon a willingness to be honest with oneself. The Emperor failed to acknowledge what he saw and, in fact, pretended not to see it at all. Failure to admit our shortcomings is one of the primary reasons we get stuck on the running wheel. How can you address what you will not acknowledge?

I believe that most of the limitations that restrain us and prevent us from achieving our desired goals are self-imposed. That is, our biggest constraints usually originate from our own habits, attitudes, responses and abilities. Have you ever heard of the Circle of Control? The Circle of Control basically proposes that, when you are looking to make progress, you

must always start with yourself and work your way outward from there. It requires that you begin by asking yourself, "What is it in me that is holding me back?" You spend more time with yourself than anyone else. You can change yourself. You have control over you actions and reactions, but, when it comes to other people and external factors, your influence is limited.

One of my mentors told me to always keep a mirror handy for self-reflection. He was right; we must be willing to take a long, hard look at ourselves because, until we do, nothing will change. Yet, looking into the mirror is only the first step. The Emperor constantly looked in the mirror, but he denied what he saw. Being aware of our faults doesn't get us very far; we must go to the next step and determine what we are going to do about them. Self-awareness and honest self-assessment are the first steps in closing the gap between where we are and where we want to go.

Another lesson that we can learn from the Emperor is about the importance of soliciting feedback. Imagine this scenario:

You're driving down a multi-lane highway and want to pass the car in front of you. You put your left turn signal on and prepare to switch lanes. You look in your rear view mirror – all clear. You check your side mirror – not a car in sight. You begin to make the change when, suddenly, a car horn blares at you. Your heart starts racing and your hands begin to tremble as you quickly swerve back into the lane you were in, barely avoiding a serious accident. Clutching the steering wheel, you realize that you almost side-swiped a car while driving 80-miles an hour. You simply didn't see it.

If you've been driving for a while, no doubt this has happened to you. There's a zone in the road that your rear and side view mirrors don't pick up. It's called a blind spot, and, if you're not careful, blind spots can kill you and others.

CEOs have blind spots, too! A blind spot is some kind of behavior that you can't see, but it exists for everyone else to see. Eliminating your personal blind spots is not much different than overcoming your driving blind spots. You must be willing to look in multiple mirrors and get input from a variety of different sources.

One of the best ways to remedy blind spots is to get feedback. Most people, however, are very reluctant to volunteer their feedback, especially when the information is negative or corrective in nature. This problem is compounded when—as in the case of the Emperor—others perceive that we are prideful, self-centered, defensive or aloof. If others believe that we will not be receptive to feedback, they usually do not offer it.

Have you ever met people who surround themselves with "yes men"? If you don't agree constantly with their point of view, they kick you out of their inner circle or label you in some way that discredits your opinion. Isn't that what the scam artists did to the Emperor and the people in his kingdom? They forewarned that any-one who couldn't see their magical fabric was either an idiot or a phony. Who wants to be identified that way? No one likes to feel foolish or unin-telligent, yet a hostile, arrogant or nonchalant response to feedback can have just that effect. People usually do one of three things in response: avoid you, talk behind your back, or lie to your face. These are all unhealthy, inef-fective responses that add time onto your sentence on the running wheel.

Unidentified blind spots can ruin your life or career! Breaking free from the running wheel requires you to be bold and honest enough to seek truthful feedback. That means others must feel comfortable openly shar-ing their opinions. A great step in the right direction is to ask people to share their insight and then cultivate your listening skills. It won't always be easy; success will require a healthy dose of humility. In the end, however, the payoff will be great. Not only will others respect you more, they also will offer feedback that is more valid and useful for gaining and maintaining your freedom from the running wheel.

The tools in this chapter are meant to help you cultivate greater self-awareness so that you can honestly assess your strengths and weaknesses and bridge the gap between your cur-rent situation and your Ideal Future.

CHAPTER TWO

There are three primary tools:

- **Self Assessment**
- **Feedback**
- **Gap Analysis (Identifying BPIs)**

We will begin with the self-assessment.

Living in the "Dash"

You've heard of the "dash" before, right? It's that little line on your tombstone that represents the years between your birth and your death. You've seen it in obituaries and on grave markers. "John Doe (1956---2010)."

That tiny, inconspicuous line looks like nothing more than a hyphen. Yet, it symbolizes all that John ever accomplished during his lifetime – what he stood for, the people he touched, even the mistakes he made.

When my nephew died, I found myself reflecting about those years represented by the dash. I thought about how quickly time seems to pass, and how precious moments slip through our fingers every day. Suddenly, I felt incredibly aware that, in that very moment, I was living out my dash and I needed to make the most of it.

What had I accomplished? Had I spent time on what mattered most? Were those who were important to me aware of how much I loved and needed them? It seemed my nephew's life was cut tragically short. How much longer would my dash last?

Each of us is living in the dash right now – somewhere between our original launch and our final landing. We encounter uncertainties along the way; the journey can be treacherous. There are peaks and valleys; mountaintops and deserts. Sometimes, the ride is so smooth you feel like you are gliding. Other times, you find yourself faced with a sharp turn when you least expect it. Then, there are those times when you don't seem to be moving at all – the stops we make in between when we get burned out, sidetracked, blind-sided or simply pause to regroup. It's all a part of the voyage.

The wonderful thing is that - even when we have to make an emergency landing or find ourselves needlessly grounded because we have been toiling on life's running wheels – we can always re-launch and continue our journey.

The next few exercises will help you to determine where you are, so that you don't take off prematurely or head in the wrong direction.

www.trailblazers-inc.com

Determining My Location Exercise
Part 1: Where am I Along the Dash?

The exercise below will help you to visualize where you are along the dash. First, fill in the year of your birth in the space provided. Next, consider the following question: "How long do you expect to live?" This is a tough question. We don't know exactly when our time will come nor do we enjoy thinking about our own mortality. Yet, it is an important question to consider. When you are ready, fill in the oldest age that you anticipate you will live to see. Finally, put an "x" on the line at the spot that marks your current age in relationship to how long you've already lived and how much longer you expect to live. Label the "x" with the current year and your current age.

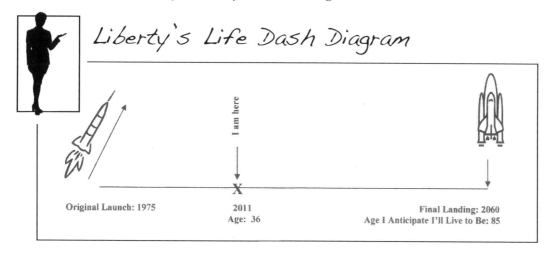

Liberty's Life Dash Diagram

I am here

Original Launch: 1975

2011
Age: 36

Final Landing: 2060
Age I Anticipate I'll Live to Be: 85

My Life Dash Diagram

Original Launch:
Year of my Birth:

"x" Marks the Spot
Where I am Along the Journey?
Year:
Age:

Final Landing:
Age I Anticipate I'll
Live to Be:

Determining My Location Exercise
Part 2: Taking Stock of Where I Am

Now review your diagram. Where are you along the dash? Are you just starting out? Are you near the middle of your life? Or perhaps nearing the end? There are stages and seasons in life. Reflect on where you are right now in the space provided.

Liberty's Thoughts Regarding the Life Dash Diagram

The diagram was an absolute eye-opener for me! I can hardly believe that nearly half of my life is probably over. I think I've dedicated so much energy to lamenting the loss of my "glory days" in Boston that I've simply allowed the last few years to slip through my fingers. I regret that I've spent so much time stuck in the past; however, I am excited that my engagement to Carl has shifted my focus to the future. I believe our relationship begins a new chapter in my life and I'm truly looking forward to the better days that are ahead.

My Thoughts Regarding My Life Dash Diagram

www.trailblazers-inc.com

Determining My Location Exercise
Part 3: Key Milestones

Think back over your life from your initial launch to where you are now. What milestone events do you recall along the way? They can be positive or negative –triumphs or tragedies. Experiences such as the death of a loved one, births, graduations, spiritual awakenings, or health challenges are all possibilities. Choose at least three significant life landmarks and note them at the appropriate places along your dash. Make a mountain peak for positive experiences and a valley for negative experiences. The stronger the impact of the experience on your life, the larger the peak or valley.

Liberty's Key Milestones

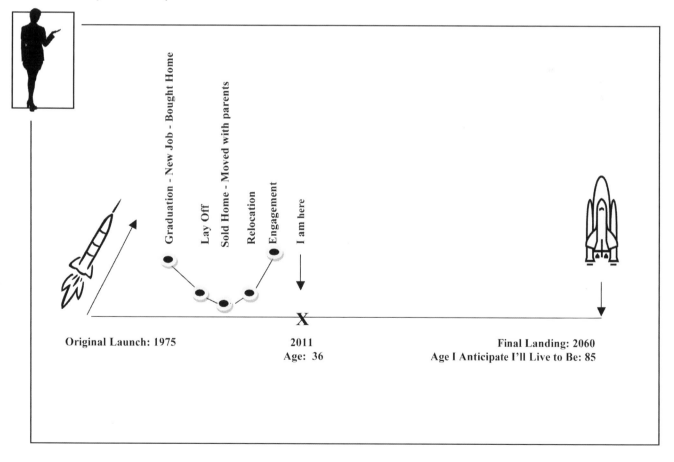

Determining My Location Exercise
Part 4: Reflecting on My Milestones

Review your peaks and valleys. How have your past experiences helped to shape your life, both positively and negatively? Do you see any patterns? Record your answers in the space provided.

Liberty's Thoughts Regarding Her Key Milestones:

I was so proud of myself when I graduated from college cum laude in 1987. I was a mediocre student in high school and struggled a bit with my writing skills during my freshman year in college, but, after a great deal of effort and discipline, I was able to earn really good grades. I landed my dream job six weeks after graduation and my career seemed

to be on the fast track until I was laid off after more than 20 years with the company. When I look back at my life, I recognize that the layoff was the first in a series of back-to-back events that took a tremendous toll on both my finances and my self-esteem. A few years later, when I was forced to move back in with my parents to avoid foreclosure on my townhouse, I suffered another devasting blow. The final milestone that damaged my self-esteem was when I moved away to Texas to accept a job for which I was greatly overqualified. Yet, looking back over the timeline, I recognize that if I had not taken the job in Houston, I would have never met my fiance. My engagement to Carl is the most wonderful milestone of them all!

My Thoughts Regarding My Key Milestones:

Where Have I Landed?

One of the most critical steps in successfully moving forward is identifying where you are emotionally. Are you soaring high, cruising along, or whirling downward in a dizzying, frightening spiral? Perhaps you aren't airborne at all. Are you grounded, taking a moment to pause so that you can refuel or repack? Maybe you're entangled in one of life's running wheels. As you prepare for your launch, it's important to accurately identify your current emotional position.

Determining My Location Exercise Part 5: My Address

Using the space provided, describe your current emotional state in life as best you can.

1. **Current Location:** Are you living at one of the running wheel "addresses" described in Chapter 1? Or are you somewhere else (i.e., soaring, crashing, simply resting, etc.)? Whatever your current location is, choose a name that accurately describes it, such as High Flyers Boulevard, Coasters Court, Crashers Way, or one of the locations from Chapter 1. Write the name you have chosen in the space provided next to the words "current location."

2. **Proof that I Live There:** Next, explain why you have selected the location that you chose. In other words, provide proof that you are residing where you say you are. For example, what evidence is there in your life that you are flying high or stuck on Complacency Lane?

3. **Events Leading Up to My Arrival:** You may have already described some of these events as milestones in the earlier exercise. Are there any other significant events that have led you to the point where you are now? If so, list them in the space next to the words "Events Leading Up to My Arrival."

4. **Pros and Cons of Relocating:** Psychologists have taught us that, until the pain of remaining the same outweighs the pain of change, most

of us will not change. Changing is hard work and we need motivation and incentives to do so. In the space provided, list the pros and cons of moving from your current emotional address. What are the benefits of staying? What negative consequences do you face if you remain where you are? List your reasons to stay put and incentives to move under the appropriate headings.

5.   **Reflection:** Finally, review all of the exercises that you have completed thus far in this chapter and reflect upon the key things that you have learned about yourself that will help you to move forward. Record them in the space provided under the words, "What I Have Learned."

Libots Emotional State:

Current Location: Limbo Avenue

My career has been stalled now for more than six years. The worst part is that I can't think of anything I am really doing to change that. All of the instability and uncertainty I've faced in the past few years have left me feeling hesitant to take a risk and pursue what I really want. It's as if I've been walking through life like a cartoon character in suspended animation. I do feel, however, that I am garnering the courage to move forward and pursue what I really want out of life.

Proof that I Live There:

My stalled career and, up until recently, my lack of a social life

Events Leading Up to My Arrival:

- *lay off*
- *forced sale of house*
- *moving back in with parents*
- *taking Houston job*

Reasons to Stay Put:

The only reason that I can think of for staying put is to play it safe.

Incentives to Move:

There are many reasons to move forward, but I think the most important one is to build my self esteem and courage.

www.trailblazers-inc.com

What I Have Learned:

What I have learned is that, instead of using my energy to move myself forward, I have spent way too much time feeling sorry for myself in the past few years. Getting engaged and working with a life coach have opened my eyes to the possibilities that lie ahead. I am willing to do what it takes to move myself forward and find greater fulfillment in both my career and personal life.

My Emotional State

Current Location:

Proof that I Live There:

Events Leading Up to My Arrival:

Reasons to Stay Put:

Incentives to Move:

What I Have Learned:

CHAPTER TWO

All is Well...Or is It?

We often only consider physical health when deciding whether or not someone is "well." Eating nutritiously and exercising are necessary for a healthy lifestyle, but these things just scratch the surface of total wellness. Wellness has many dimensions. It is exemplified by quality of life and a sense of well being. In the exercise that follows, you will complete a Wellness Wheel.

As we mentioned previously, ME, Inc. consists of several interdependent divisions that comprise your overall health. They include: physical health and wellness; career and professional development; finances and wealth; spiritual well being; friends and family; lifelong learning and personal growth; and recreation and fun.

A balanced life is one where you spread your energy and effort among key areas of importance. When there is a degree of balance among different areas, you experience a sense of well being and fulfillment. On the other hand, it's easy to find yourself "off balance" when life is busy or all of your energy is focused solely on one area.

Taking time to look at your life from a helicopter view can help bring things back into balance. The next exercise, the Wellness Wheel, helps you to consider each critical life division in turn so that you can assess what's off balance. In doing so, you can identify areas that need more attention.

www.trailblazers-inc.com

Wellness Wheel Exercise
Part 1: And the Survey Says...

This exercise focuses upon eight areas that, together, comprise the life divisions of ME, Inc. Each question measures your level of satisfaction in a particular area at this given time. As you work through this assessment, you will find areas where you can acknowledge yourself for the success you have created and areas where you may want to improve your level of satisfaction. Rank each statement on a scale from 5 (always) to 1 (never), then total your scores for each area.

CATEGORIES	Your Rating				
FITNESS & HEALTH *Eat, Sleep, Exercise, Physical Appearance*	5 always	4 often	3 some-times	2 rarely	1 never
1) **I get a minimum of 30 minutes of vigorous exercise five days a week.**					
2) **I regularly eat a healthy breakfast and take time to prepare balanced meals.**					
3) **I drink at least 8 glasses of water per day.**					
4) **I get an annual physical, visit the dentist, and take recommended screening tests.**					
5) **I have the energy and focus I need to meet my daily challenges.**					
6) **I avoid junk food and eating on the run.**					
7) **I maintain a healthy weight for my height and build.**					
8) **I get 7-8 hours of sleep at least 5 nights a week.**					
9) **I drink fewer than 5 alcoholic drinks per week and less than 5 soft drinks per week.**					
10) **I am satisfied with my overall physical appearance.**					
Total Score *(Health & Fitness):* = _____ /50					

CAREER & PROFESSIONAL DEVELOPMENT *Career Direction, Professional Growth Opportunities, Alignment of Career with Values, Temperament, Natural Talents*	Your Ratings				
	5 always	4 often	3 some- times	2 rarely	1 never
1) I have access to ample opportunities for growth and learning in my career.					
2) I am making real and visible contributions that allow me to feel successful and rewarded in my work.					
3) My career brings meaning and value to my life.					
4) I am satisfied with my present level of performance and accomplishment in my work.					
5) I am satisfied with the compensation that I receive for my work.					
6) I feel the work I do enhances the well-being of others.					
7) My work affords me an opportunity to use my strengths and gifts on a daily basis.					
8) I am satisfied with the pace of my career growth.					
9) My work challenges me in a healthy way.					
10) I enjoy my work.					

Total Score *(Career & Professional Development)*: = _____ /50

WEALTH & FINANCES *Give, Save, Invest, Spend*	Your Ratings				
	5 always	4 often	3 some- times	2 rarely	1 never
1) I keep my financial documents (bills, insurance policies, paperwork for investments, deeds, wills, etc.) in an orderly, organized fashion so that they are easy to locate.					
2) I keep at least three to six months' worth of living expenses set aside in case of an emergency.					
3) I have enough discretionary income to enjoy leisure, recreation and travel activities.					
4) I make charitable contributions as a way of giving back to the community or causes I strongly believe in.					
5) I set aside a percentage of my income to work toward my long-term financial goals, such as saving for a down payment on a home, investing for my child's college education and retirement.					
6) I make enough money to meet my basic expenditures.					
7) I live within my means and budget my spending each month.					
8) I resist buying unnecessary items on impulse.					
9) I pay my bills on time.					
10) I maintain a strong credit rating and comfortable level of debt and monitor both consistently.					

Total Score *(Wealth & Finances)*: = _____ /50

SPIRITUALITY *Reflection, Awareness, Meaning, Purpose*	Your Ratings				
	5 always	4 often	3 some- times	2 rarely	1 never
1) Prayer, meditation, and/or quiet personal reflection is/are important in my life.					
2) I am comfortable with my spiritual life, personal values and beliefs, and feel at ease when speaking with others about them.					
3) There is a direct relationship between my spiritual beliefs, personal values and daily actions.					
4) My spiritual beliefs and values offer me hope and direction, especially during challenging times.					
5) Life is meaningful for me; I know the unique purpose for which I was created and am living it out.					
6) I am a spiritual person.					
7) I have a strong sense of hope and optimism in my life and try to encourage others in life-affirming ways.					
8) I wake up each day with a sense of eager anticipation.					
9) I am consistently striving to grow spiritually and I see it as a lifelong process.					
10) I am grateful for the blessings and "miracles" in my daily life.					

Total Score *(Spirituality)* = _____ /50

PERSONAL DEVELOPMENT & GROWTH *Education, Learning, Self Awareness*	Your Ratings				
	5 always	4 often	3 some- times	2 rarely	1 never
1) I understand myself and my needs.					
2) Although I recognize that I still have work to do, I like myself and am comfortable with who I am.					
3) I learn from my mistakes and failures and move on.					
4) My personal life is positive and I am a fulfilled person.					
5) I pursue both formal and informal learning opportunities.					
6) I say "no" to things that are less important in life so that I can have time for the things that are most important to me.					
7) I regularly learn new skills, meet new people and try new things.					
8) I am becoming more and more of the person I desire to be.					
9) I seek and accept feedback from others regarding how well I am doing in various aspects of my life.					
10) I perceive problems as opportunities for growth.					

Total Score *(Personal Development & Growth)*: _____ /50

FAMILY & FRIENDS *Relationships, Time, Quality, Support*	Your Ratings				
	5 always	4 often	3 some- times	2 rarely	1 never
1) I have fulfilling relationships with a network of loving and supportive friends and family.					
2) I spend the right amount of time with my family and friends.					
3) My relationships are fairly and equally balanced.					
4) I have at least one person available to me who really listens and that I can confide in regarding personal matters.					
5) I share my true feelings and life dreams with the people closest to me.					
6) I deliver on my promises to others, no matter what they are.					
7) My words and actions reinforce my personal brand promise.					
8) I know what it means to love unconditionally and do so.					
9) My family and close friends know that I love them because I express it in a way that is meaningful to them.					
10) I feel good about the degree of closeness that I have with my friends and family.					
Total Score *(Friends & Family)*: _____/50					

RECREATION & FUN *Leisure, Hobbies, Passions, Laughter*	Your Ratings				
	5 always	4 often	3 some- times	2 rarely	1 never
1) I include a healthy dose of fun and recreation in my life.					
2) Humor, laughter, and playfulness are a part of my daily life.					
3) I find positive ways to deal with stress. (i.e., exercise, talking, meditating, etc.)					
4) When life feels "out of control," I choose healthy behaviors to help me re-center and renew (i.e., I do not use shopping, eating, sleeping, television/ internet, drugs or other substances to escape and cope).					
5) I take time to relax and refresh myself.					
6) I live my life with passion and joy.					
7) I regularly attend social events and activities.					
8) I am enjoying life; I do something fun at least once a week.					
9) I readily shift from a goal-oriented frame of mind to a "purposeless" activity when it is appropriate to do so.					
10) My work and personal life are well balanced.					
Total Score *(Recreation & Fun)*: _____/50					

PHYSICAL ENVIRONMENT *Home & Work Environment, Location, Community*	Your Ratings				
	5 always	4 often	3 some- times	2 rarely	1 never
1) I work to actively improve and beautify my physical surroundings, both at home and at work.					
2) My home environment and furnishings allow me to feel hospitable and welcoming.					
3) My home environment promotes a sense of peace, love, and security.					
4) My work space is clean, efficient, and pleasing to my senses.					
5) I feel a sense of belonging in the community where I live.					
6) I have options in the community where I live to do the things I love to do.					
7) I believe that I am living in the geographical location where I am supposed to be.					
8) The level of order in my home surroundings is appropriate to my needs.					
9) I feel at home in my house and enjoy being there.					
10) I feel safe in my neighborhood.					
Total Score *(Physical Environment)*: _____ /50					

Optional Sections

If you wish, you may separate any of the divisions above into departments so that you can take a closer look at a more specific area of your life. You may either devise your own questionnaire to reflect your new subcategory or simply rate the subcategory on a scale of 10-50 to reflect your level of satisfaction with it.

For your convenience, I have included questionnaires for three departments. The first two departments – parenting and spouse/significant other - are related to the family/friends division.

The third department is related to the physical well-being and fitness division. It's physical appearance. Feel free to complete the questionnaires if they represent areas of significance to you. Because the questionnaires for the departments only contain five questions (instead of 10), you will need to multiply the total you get from adding the columns by two. Feel free to divide the department of parenting even further into units if you wish to reflect your relationship with each of your children.

SUB-CATEGORIES	Your Ratings				
	5 always	4 often	3 some-times	2 rarely	1 never

PARENTING
Communication, Respect, Involvement

	5	4	3	2	1
1) I am satisfied with the role that I play and the contributions that I make in my children's lives.					
2) My children and I have free, open and honest dialogue.					
3) I feel respected and admired by my children.					
4) I make myself available to my children and spend quality, caring time with them.					
5) I respect my children as complete human beings at all stages of life, and adjust my parenting style to accommodate their growth and development as they mature.					

Total Score *(Parenting)*: _____/50*
Don't forget to add each column together and multiply the total by two to get your score.

SPOUSE/SIGNIFICANT OTHER	Your Ratings				
Communication, Romance, Intimacy/Connectedness	5 always	4 often	3 some-times	2 rarely	1 never
1) I can confide in my spouse/significant other.					
2) I spend adequate time with spouse/significant other.					
3) I feel supported by my spouse/significant other.					
4) I feel my spouse/significant other and I have a sufficient amount of romance in our relationship.					
5) I am satisfied with the amount of intimacy and physical contact between me and my spouse/significant other.					

Total Score *(Spouse/Significant Other)*: _____/50*
Don't forget to add each column together and multiply the total by two to get your score.

PHYSICAL APPEARANCE	Your Ratings				
Wardrobe, Grooming, General Appearance	5 always	4 often	3 some-times	2 rarely	1 never
1. I am generally satisfied with my overall appearance and grooming.					
2. My wardrobe and grooming are in alignment with my personal brand promise and clearly express who I am.					
3. I take care to ensure my hair and fingernails are clean and adequately groomed.					
4. I consider the environment and occasion when selecting my wardrobe.					
5. I love the way I groom myself and the clothes that I wear.					

Total Score *(Physical Appearance)*: _____/50*
Don't forget to add each column together and multiply the total by two to get your score.

Wellness Wheel Exercise
Part 2: Tallying the Scores

To get a snapshot of your life, record your total scores from Part 1 in the table provided.

Liberty's Wellness Table

Category	Score
Fitness & Health	25
Career & Professional Development	20
Wealth & Finances	19
Spirituality	40
Personal Development & Growth	33
Friends & Family	22
Fun & Recreation	39
Physical Environment	38
Sub-category/Category	**Score**
Fiancé/Friends & Family	48
Physical Appearance/Fitness & Health	44

www.trailblazers-inc.com

My Wellness Table

Category	Score
Fitness & Health	
Career & Professional Development	
Wealth & Finances	
Spirituality	
Personal Development & Growth	
Friends & Family	
Fun & Recreation	
Physical Environment	
Subcategory/Category	Score
Parenting/Friends & Family	
Spouse/Significant Other/Friends & Family	
Physical Appearance/Fitness & Health	
Other (please specify):	
Other (please specify):	
Other (please specify):	
Other (please specify):	
Other (please specify):	

Wellness Wheel Exercise
Part 3: Plotting My Scores

When you are done, transfer your scores onto the Wellness Wheel by completing the following steps:

1. Find the categories on the wheel that you have broken down into departments. Divide those categories into the appropriate number of segments and label those segments accordingly.

2. Take the scores from the table and transfer them to the Wellness Wheel by drawing an arc at the appropriate place along each line to indicate your score for the corresponding category or sub-category.

Liberty's Wellness Wheel

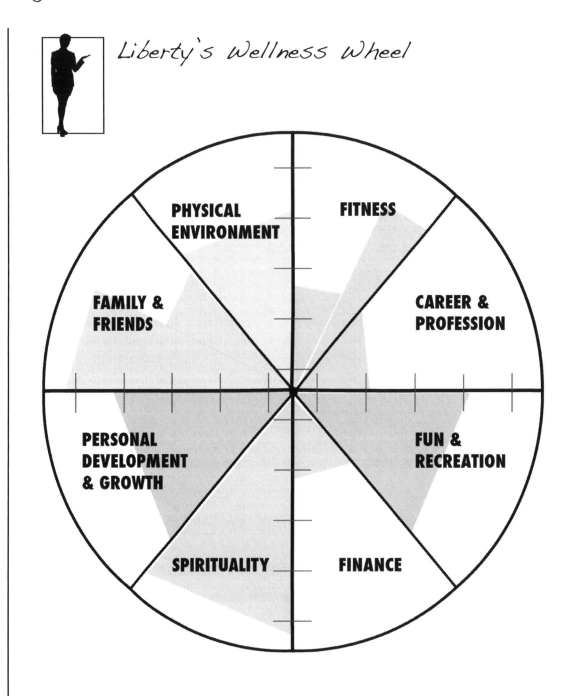

My Wellness Wheel

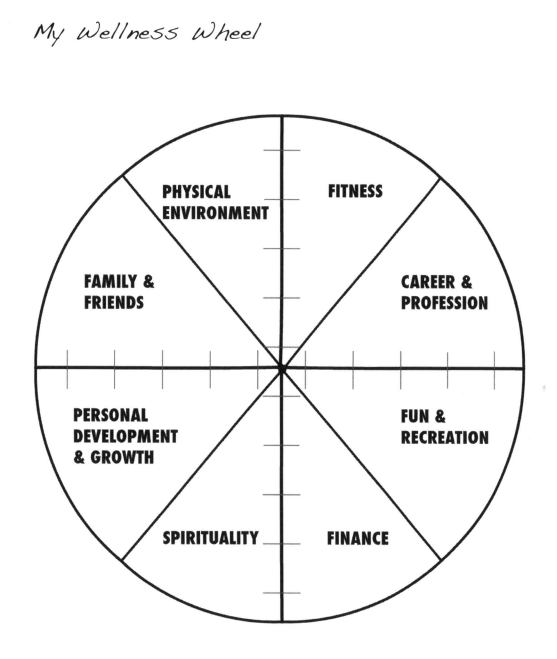

CHAPTER TWO

Wellness Wheel Exercise
Part 4: A Bumpy Ride?

Look at your completed wheel. The new perimeter of the circle represents your Wellness Wheel. If your life is riding on this wheel, how bumpy is the ride? Answer the following questions to help you increase your satisfaction and life balance.

www.trailblazers-inc.com

Liberty's Observations about Her Wellness Wheel

1. **How do you feel about your life overall as you look at your wheel?** *Overall, I have a few areas that are doing well right now and providing me with the motivation to try and work on the other areas. My strongest area, of course, is my relationship with my fiancé. Since he came into my life, I have definitely been having more fun and taking time for recreation. He has also encouraged me to learn more about Houston and I have come to love the city. I have even been a bit more conscientious about my appearance. I have always been a deeply spiritual person, so that is my second strongest category. I am working to focus on what is going right these days so that I can break out of the rut that I have been in and work on my career and financial stability.*

2. **Are there any surprises for you?** *Yes, I was surprised at how low family and friends scored. I am truly a family-oriented person, but I realized when I looked at my wheel that I haven't stayed in touch very well since I moved. I would like to do better with that.*

3. **What area(s) on the wheel is in most desperate need of change?** *Wealth and finances; career and professional development, and friends and family.*

4. **What is the current state of this area(s)?** *They are all suffering from neglect.*

5. **What is missing or not working for you in this area(s)?** *I need to develop a strategy for how to intentionally recover in each of those areas. Each of them has suffered as a result of my tendency to bury my head in the sand over the past few years.*

6. **What would you like to create in this area(s)?** *I would like repair, revive and reconnect. I would like to repair my finances, revive my career, and reconnect with my family.*

7. **How could you make space for these changes?** *For me, I don't think it's a matter of finding the time…it's a matter of simply making the effort.*

8. **What help and cooperation from others might you need?** *I will definitely need the loving support of my fiancé and the forgiveness of my family and friends. I recognize that I have been somewhat distant these past few years.*

My Obervations about My Wellness Wheel

1. How do you feel about your life overall as you look at your Wheel?

2. Are there any surprises for you?

3. What area(s) on the wheel is in most desperate need of change?

4. What is the current state of this area(s)?

5. What is missing or not working for you in this area(s)?

6. What would you like to create in this area(s)?

7. How could you make space for these changes?

8. What help and cooperation from others might you need?

CHAPTER TWO

Finishing Touches
Self Assessment Checklist

If you answered "no" to any of the checklist questions, go back and redo the appropriate portion(s) of your self assessment.

Y	N	Have you been completely honest with yourself about…
		your emotions?
		your past?
		the role that you've played in your successes and failures?
		the overall status of your life, as well as where things stand in your specific life divisions?

Setting aside time to meditate and reflect on a consistent basis is a critical key to success. Purchase a journal and find a quiet place to lock yourself away at least once a month so that you can reflect about your "Dash." Be sure to include one new achievement and one target for change in each journal entry.

Words to Live By

"This above all: to thine own self be true."

\- William Shakespeare (Hamlet)

www.trailblazers-inc.com

What Others See
When They See "Me"

While self-assessment is essential, it is also important to get information about yourself from outside sources. Feedback is one of the most effective tools that you can use to learn about yourself. Good intentions alone are not enough. Even if you mean well, your impact is weakened if others misunderstand or misperceive your intent. Gathering feedback can help you to understand what people think about you, your style of interacting, and your approach. This information can help you close the gap between your intentions and the resulting outcome. Feedback also helps to reduce your blind spots. Hearing what others think about you can help identify strengths and weaknesses that you haven't noticed before or have been reluctant to acknowledge.

The next two exercises are tools for soliciting feedback. Each of the exercises takes a different approach to gaining insight from others. I recommend that you complete both of the exercises so that you can collect as much information as possible. Exercise number one requires you to contact at least five people to solicit their opinions about your greatest strengths and weaknesses. The second exercise requires you to send out the relationship letters and personal brand promise that you wrote in Chapter 1

and solicit feedback on them.

Gathering honest feedback is not easy. It requires openness, humility and self-control on your part. Many people have become skeptical about sharing their views and opinions openly with others because of the reactions that they have received in the past. The fear of reprisal and hurt feelings are among the primary concerns. In order to overcome this, you must ask yourself if you are truly willing to hear what others have to say. Remember, if you are genuinely seeking the truth, you may not hear what you want to hear. If your reaction is perceived as being defensive, arrogant or aloof, you will severely weaken your chances of getting honest feedback now and in the future.

I suggest you let those that you are soliciting feedback from know why you are doing the exercise. Inform them of your intent to create a Strategic Life Plan that will guide your personal development and help you find greater fulfillment. Let them know that only honest feedback will help you in your quest and that you value their opinion.

Give yourself space and time to process feedback. No matter how tough you are and how much you value others' opinions, receiving feedback can provoke an emotional response. You may experience denial, you may become argumentative, or you may feel hurt or frustrated. Give yourself time to integrate the emotions that arise when facing a critique. Set the feedback aside. Take a walk, exercise, talk it out with a friend, or jot some notes about how you feel. Then, come back to the feedback and process it. Whatever you do, don't punish people for giving you feedback. Be open to and appreciative of all of the feedback received, whether you agree with it or not. At the very least, it will provide you with greater insight into how people perceive you.

Are you ready? Let's carry on with the difficult assignment of learning what others think of you.

www.trailblazers-inc.com

Feedback Exercise Part 1: Strengths and Weaknesses Poll

This exercise walks you through the steps of soliciting feedback from others regarding what they perceive to be your greatest strengths and weaknesses.

1. **Choose Five People:** Identify at least five people who know you well. Try to select people who know you in different ways. These may be family members, friends, colleagues, neighbors, customers, or anyone who interacts with you on a regular basis. The more diverse the group, the better.

2. **Reach Out to Request Their Participation:** Contact each of these people to let them know that you are working on completing a Strategic Life Plan to assist you in your personal growth and development and that you need their honest feedback. (Emphasize that, in order to be helpful, the feedback must be truthful). Tell them that you are inviting them to complete a brief survey with seven open-ended questions regarding your strengths and weaknesses. Explain when the responses are due and ask if they are willing to participate.

3. **Distribute & Collect the Surveys:** Distribute the survey, along with a reminder of the deadline and instructions on how to return the survey once it has been completed. E-mail is a quick and easy way to distribute

and collect surveys; however, if you prefer to increase the anonymity, you have at least two options. The first is to distribute self-addressed stamped envelopes to respondents so that they can return their responses anonymously through the mail. The second is to use Survey Monkey (surveymonkey.com) or some equivalent to create an online survey that can be returned anonymously. Such services are easy to use and provided free or for a nominal fee.

4. **Analyze the Results:** You will analyze the results from this survey along with the findings from Exercise 2. Instructions for analyzing the feedback from both exercises are listed at the end of the section.

Feedback Exercise Part 2: Personal Strengths and Weaknesses Poll

1. Describe your first impression of me. How has your perception of me changed over time?

2. On a scale of 1-10 (with 10 being the highest), how would you rate my ability to effectively communicate with you? What do you particularly like about my communication style? What would you like to see me change?

3. Express what you would describe as my greatest strength. What specific examples do you have of times that you witnessed me display that strength?

CHAPTER TWO

4. What areas do you think I need to pay closer attention to as I endeavor to become a better person? Share specific examples of times that you think I could have improved my behavior or should have done something differently.

5. What can you always depend on me for?

6. In what ways do you wish you could rely on me more?

7. What do you think should be my top personal development goal for this upcoming year?

Feedback Exercise
Part 3: To the Letter

In the last chapter, you created a Personal Brand Promise and wrote letters from the key people in your life describing the impact that you would like to make upon their lives. During this exercise, you are going to seek outside feedback as a part of your reality check.

1. **Copy the Letters:** First, you will need to make copies of the letters you wrote for the "Letters from the Future" exercise.

2. **Distribute the Letters & Your Brand Promise:** The next step is to send a copy of each letter to the person that it was written about, along with a copy of your Personal Brand Promise and the feedback questions that follow.

3. **Request Feedback:** Ask each letter recipient to provide you with honest feedback to the questions that follow.

Feedback Exercise Part 4: Letters to the Future and Personal Brand Promise

1. How well do the claims made in my Personal Brand Promise match the characteristics of my relationship with you?

2. Which part(s) of my Personal Brand Promise rings most true for you? Which part(s) of my Personal Brand Promise contradicts or challenges your perception of me?

3. Tell me about your initial impression when reading the Letter to the Future that I wrote about our relationship.

4. How well does the picture painted in the Letter to the Future match what you are currently experiencing in the relationship that we share?

5. What do you see as the greatest benefit(s) of having a relationship with me?

6. What do I need to work on in order to fulfill the vision painted in the Letter to the Future?

7. What additional advice do you have for how I might improve our relationship?

CHAPTER TWO

Feedback Exercise
Part 5: Analyzing My Feedback

Now that you have received feedback on what others perceive to be your greatest strengths and weaknesses, it is time to analyze it.

1. **First Review:** Start by reading all of your feedback for the first time. After you have read through it once, jot some notes about how you feel. Try to fend off defensiveness and be as open-minded as possible. Set the feedback aside until at least the next day.

2. **Second Review:** After some time and space, when you feel a bit more objective, take a second look at the feedback. Try not to get bogged down in the details. At this point, you are simply looking for the big picture; you are trying to get a sense of what, in general, you do well and what, in general, you don't do as well. Look for commonalities across the individuals who provided you with feedback. Create themes around those commonalities. When you are ready, respond objectively to the questions that follow.

Freeman's Responses

In general, people see my strengths as:
- *dependable*
- *even-tempered*
- *humble*
- *resourceful*
- *tendency to think before speaking*
- *kind*

In general, people see my areas in need of development as:
- *tendency to neglect my own needs and self-care*
- *being too cautious and risk adverse*
- *needing to have more fun and laugh more often*
- *being overcritical of myself*
- *having an inclination to analyze everything*

What most surprised me was:

- *People perceive me as not laughing and having enough fun. I think I have a great (perhaps somewhat dry) sense of humor, and although I primarily focused on kid-friendly vacations and activities while I was raising my children, I found the trips and family days we've shared over the past few years to be quite enjoyable.*

My Responses

In general, people see my strengths as:

-

-

-

-

-

In general, people see my areas in need of development as:

-

-

-

-

-

CHAPTER TWO

What most surprised me was:

-

-

-

-

-

-

3. **Perception Comparison:** The next step is to compare the perception of others with your own perception. Using the diagram provided on page 139, compare your self-assessment to the feedback you received by grouping your identified strengths and areas in need of development into four categories:

   a. **Areas of strength** where your self-assessment overlapped with your feedback from others (i.e., you both identified these areas as strengths);

   b. **Areas in need of development** where your self-assessment overlapped with your feedback from others (i.e., you both identified these areas as being in need of development);

   c. **Areas that those who gave you feedback saw as strengths** that you either identified as areas in need of development or did not identify at all (i.e., your feedback from others identified these areas as strengths, although you did not list them at all or saw them as areas in need of development); and

   d. **Areas that those who gave you feedback saw as areas in need of development** and you either saw as strengths or did not identify at all (i.e., your feedback from others identified these areas as ones in need of development, although you identified them as strengths or did not identify them at all).

Freeman's Perception Comparison

Areas of Strength (according to self and others)	Areas in Need of Development (according to self and others)
-dependability -self control -resourcefulness -compassion -determination	-focus on self -social life with adults my age
Areas of Strength (according to others) -humility -thinking before speaking	**Areas in Need of Development (according to others)** -sense of adventure and fun -self criticism -overanalyzing

My Perception Comparison

Areas of Strength (according to self and others)	Areas in Need of Development (according to self and others)
Areas of Strength (according to others)	**Areas in Need of Development (according to others)**

Identifying Areas for Improvement Exercise
Part 1: My Big Picture Issues

Re-read your answers to the self assessment exercises (Where am I Along the Dash?; Key Milestones; Where Have I Landed?; Current Address; and Wellness Wheel), and review the feedback that you received from others once again. This time look for themes and commonalities. What big, broad critical life issues emerge? These are called Big Picture Issues (BPIs).

What BPIs have been identified by you and/or others that, if effectively addressed, would improve your life significantly? Write down the life-changing BPIs that surfaced for you during this chapter. List as many as you can think of in the space provided.

Freeman's BPIs

- ENJOY THE JOURNEY: *Relax, loosen up and laugh a bit more, do something spontaneous.*

- FOCUS ON FREEMAN: *Remember that it's my time now. Do things that I enjoy simply because I enjoy them. Don't be so hard on myself.*

- HEALTH AND PHYSICAL FITNESS: *Pay attention to my health and take better care of myself.*

- FOLLOW MY HEART: *Learn to be creative and go with my gut instinct sometimes. Try not to over think and overanalyze things.*

- ENTREPRENERSHIP: *Don't be paralyzed by the fear of early retirement. Focus on becoming the entrepreneur that I've always wanted to be. Push myself out of my comfort zone and explore the possibilities.*

- FAMILY AND FRIENDS: *My children have matured into young adults. Enjoy this new season of independence in their lives and shower my grandchildren with love and affection. Reconnect with old friends and be open to finding new ones.*

My BPIs

Identifying Areas for Improvement Exercise
Part 2: More Big Picture Issues

Review your list of BPIs. Does something seem to be missing? If so, go back and add to your list until you feel that it is fairly comprehensive.

Freeman's Additional BPI

EXPLORING NEW ADVENTURES: *So much of my life has revolved around my children and preparing them for adulthood that I have lost touch with other adults. Now is the time for me to explore new adventures, particularly relationships (perhaps even one that is romantic in nature). I would also like to explore new hobbies and places to visit.*

Finishing Touches

Soliciting Feedback Checklist

Y	N	Have you…
		avoided becoming defensive?
		asked for specific advice on what to do differently and what to repeat going forward?
		accepted the impact of your behavior as reality for the other person? (Remember, you don't have to agree.)
		asked clarifying questions, if needed?
		thanked everyone who participated for taking the time to respond?
		thought about how you will try out some of the suggestions?

Push yourself to solicit feedback on a regular basis. For loved ones who have difficulty expressing themselves, try posing specific questions and having them write down their responses in a journal before sharing their answers with you. This gives your loved ones time to prepare for discussions in a thoughtful manner and may be less intimidating for those who are uncomfortable with conflict.

Words to Live By

"Feedback is the breakfast of champions."

–Ken Blanchard

Conclusion

This was a tough chapter. You held up a mirror and dug deep to "Reveal the Truth" about yourself and your current location. As difficult as it is to honestly assess yourself and open yourself up to feedback, it is well worth it. With a solid understanding of where you want to go, where you are right now and the BPIs that stand between the two, you are ready to address another crucial question, "How Do I Get from Where I am to Where I Desire to Go?" We will begin considering the answer in the next chapter as you "Explore Your Options."

CHAPTER TWO

Countdown to Launch

Chart your progress by shading in the
steps that you have completed.

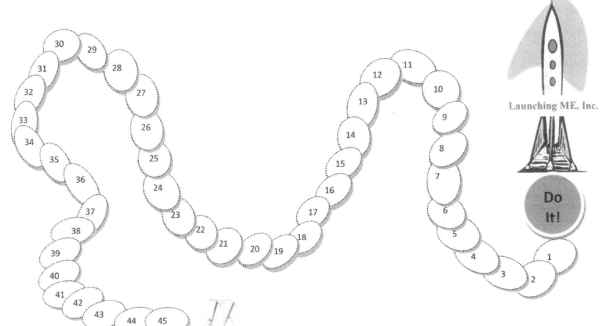

Launching ME, Inc.

Do It!

45-Core Values	23-From - To
44-Legacy and Mission	22-SWOT Matrix
43-Epitaph	21-TOWS Matrix
42-Eulogy	20-Success Indicators
41-Mission Statement	19-Annual Benchmarks
40-Choose Planning Horizon	18-Annual Theme
39-Vision Statement	17-Quarterly Targets
38-Critical Success Factors	16-M&Ms
37-Affirmations	15-One Page Life Plan
36-Self-Lead Skills Inventory	14-My Rewards List
35-Communication Styles Test	13-SMARTer Goals
34-Personal Brand	12-Weekly Plan
33-Personal Brand Logo	11-Weekly Schedule
32-Roles and Relationships	10-Today's Goals
31-Letters from the Future	9-Prioritized To Do list
30-Where Am I Along the Dash?	8-Support/Accountability
29-Wellness Wheel Part I	7-Habits to Break/Make
28-Wellness Wheel Part II	6-Payoff Matrix
27-Personal Strengths/Weaknesses	5-Habit You Will Focus On
26-To the Letter	4-Identifying Motivation
25-Perception Comparison	3-Obstacles/Triggers
24-BPIs	2-Support System
	1-Affirmation

EXPLORE YOUR OPTIONS

CONSIDERING THE POSSIBLITIES

"There are those who look at things the way they are, and ask why... I dream of things that never were, and ask why not?"

- Robert F. Kennedy

Which Way Should I Go?

You have identified your destination and determined your starting point. Now, it's time to consider how you want to get there. In addition to the map, there is another navigational tool that I consistently use – the Global Positioning System or GPS. It is a bit more interactive than a map. I type in where I want to go and it offers some options regarding which route I prefer to take. Do I want to travel the fastest way or go the shortest distance? Am I trying to avoid highways, u-turns or tolls? Would I like to steer clear of traffic? There are countless alternatives to consider when determining which route is best for me.

The same holds true for strategic planning. After my clients have analyzed the terrain that lies between where they are and where they want to go, I work with them to brainstorm possibilities for closing the gap. CEOs think outside the box. They're creative, and usually have a reputation for exploring until no stone is left unturned. They rarely take the first idea that comes to mind. As the CEO of ME, Inc., you are not limiting your options at this point; you are exploring as many as you can.

There are many possible ways for you to close the gap between the Ideal Future that you have identified for ME, Inc. and the current reality that you discovered in the last chapter. It is time to consider your choices for moving forward. In this chapter, you will tackle the third step in the F.R.E.E.D. Coaching Model – EXPLORE YOUR OPTIONS. You will use brainstorming tools to come up with ways to move closer to your desired destination.

As you explore the possibilities, you will undoubtedly find that each option has its pros and cons. For example, you might choose the shortest distance simply to discover yourself driving down busy streets with loads of traffic lights. Or, you might decide to avoid the tolls only to find that you have to drive miles out of the way to do so.

Lots of people will have an opinion about which path is best for you. Some will prefer the scenic route while others will love short cuts. Town natives will argue for hours about the best way to get from one side of the city to the other. In the end, however, you will have to live with the consequences of your choices. Ultimately, you must decide which path is right for you.

This chapter will not only tap into your creativity to brainstorm solutions, it will also equip you to narrow the field and make an informed choice about how to best move forward. It will position you one step closer to the launch of ME, Inc.

www.trailblazers-inc.com

It Matters Which Way I Go

In Lewis Carroll's Alice in Wonderland, young Alice inquires of the Cheshire Cat:

"Would you tell me, please, which way I ought to go from here?"

"That depends a good deal on where you want to get to," replies the cat.

"I don't much care where," says Alice.

"Then it doesn't much matter which way you go," says the cat.

I love to go for walks, especially on crisp autumn days. I enjoy the feeling of the wind bristling through my hair and the sun warming my skin. On cool fall mornings, I will often grab my jacket and hit the street. I usually don't have a particular destination in mind, so my route tends to be quite spontaneous. Sometimes, I walk towards the park. Other times, I wander in the direction of the mall. Occasionally, something random intrigues me—like hearing the sound of geese in the distance or catching a glimpse of leaves falling to the ground – and I veer off of the path that I am on to explore what has caught my attention. Those are days when, like Alice, I really don't care much where I am headed. I am simply looking to enjoy the experience of being outdoors.

Leading my life in such a laissez-faire manner on a daily basis, however, would get me into trouble. CEOs have a strategic approach to life—they know who they are, what they value, where they are headed, and how they intend to get there. They understand that, if you do care where you're going, it matters very much which way you go.

Plotting My Strategy

Now, it's time to brainstorm strategies for moving forward. A strategy is a major course of action that deliberately leads toward the achievement of your vision and mission. Evaluating and selecting the right strategy is like planning a trip. There are many decisions to make. You start with the most critical questions. First, you consider the nature and purpose of your trip – where you are going and why. In other words, you begin by asking yourself, "What is my intended destination and what do I hope to accomplish during this journey?"

Before proceeding any further with the decision-making process, you also must consider your resources. That is, you ask yourself, "What do I have to work with? How much time, money and effort am I willing to allocate for this trip?" These three major factors - your destination, your purpose, and your resources - serve as reference points for the remainder of your choices.

With these major questions out to the way, you are ready to brainstorm some possibilities. You begin to tackle other issues, such as who to bring along, when to leave, what type of clothes to pack, and how you will get there. Taking everything into consideration, you find that a number of plausible solutions exist. Each possibility has its strong points. One seems more fun. Another appears more practical. These routes are faster. Those are more scenic. Faced with a myriad of possibilities, you revisit the three big questions: Where am I going? What do I hope to accomplish? And what are my resources? You weigh your options against one another in context of those answers. You think about the variations, combinations and alternatives. You narrow down your list, sometimes sacrificing one desire for another. Finally, you settle on the options that seem best suited to your destination, purpose, and resources.

You are about to go through a similar process now as you brainstorm possibilities to move you forward. By the end of this chapter, you will have selected three to five BPIs to target, along with several strategies designed to bring you closer to the accomplishment of your mission and vision over your planning horizon.

Deciding Where to Focus

Let's begin by deciding where you would like to focus. At the end of Chapter Two, you brainstormed a list of BPI's that, if addressed, would improve the quality of your life. It would be great if you could annihilate every obstacle that is blocking your way in one fell swoop. Experience has taught me, however, that it just doesn't work that way. You will have a much better chance of getting where you want to go if you prioritize and focus. Once you've made some headway chipping away at the first few issues, you can go back to your list and pick another one or two to work on, and so on.

Choosing a Strategy Exercise
Part 1: Comparing BPIs

Review the BPIs on your list again. This time, use the grid provided to rank each BPI relative to four categories: 1) importance, 2) feasibility, 3) resources, and 4) leverage. An explanation of each category follows.

Importance:

Your focus should be on the BPIs that will have the most significant impact on your life. It is foolish to waste time, energy and other resources improving in areas that don't really matter much. Does this BPI have a significant influence on your ability to accomplish your mission, fulfill your vision, live out your core values, and deliver on your brand promise? Is it impeding you from taking advantage of significant opportunities or utilizing your gifts, talents and strengths fully? Must you address this issue to consider yourself successful or is it simply something that is nice to do? Remind yourself of why you want to tackle this BPI. Starting with areas that are a top priority will keep you more focused and motivated than beginning with those that are just interesting or nice to do.

Feasibility:

The category of feasibility explores how likely it is that you will be able to make significant improvements or achievements in a particular area. There are three considerations associated with feasibility: 1) degree of control; 2) level of motivation; and 3) level of commitment.

First of all, it is important that you select areas that you believe you are able to impact or change. Be realistic. Can you identify things that you can actually do and control to influence your progress in this particular area? The more influence you believe you can exert over changing a particular area, the more feasible it is.

Another consideration under feasibility is your motivation level related to the area. You must be able to find something about an area that motivates or excites you, even if that motivation simply is being rid of the challenge that this area represents. The more motivated you are to change in a given area, the higher the feasibility.

Finally, feasibility takes into consideration how committed you are to seeing change in a particular area. Are you willing to do whatever it takes? The

CHAPTER THREE

more committed you are, the more feasible it is that you will see improvement in the area.

Resources:

You will need to commit some resources to addressing your BPIs. Those resources may include time, money, external support, and so on. Expending resources in one area means you will have fewer resources to allocate to another area. The bottom line is that you will have to make sacrifices. When rating an area in the category of resources, remember that 5 means very little resource allocation is needed and 1 means a great deal of resources are required.

Leverage:

Leverage involves determining which actions and changes offer the greatest return on investment. High leverage areas are those areas that, if addressed effectively, have the greatest potential to lead to significant, enduring improvements while maximizing your resources. Leverage involves looking at connections among different areas and finding intersecting points that, when activated, spur a chain reaction. When rating an area in the category of leverage, rate its potential impact on the other BPIs. The more links you can find between an issue and other key areas, the greater the leverage.

Freeman's BPI Comparison Chart

Big Picture Issue (BPI)	Importance	Feasibility	Resources	Leverage	Total
Enjoy the Journey	5	5	3	5	**18**
Focus on Freeman	4	4	5	4	**17**
Improve Health and Physical Fitness	5	3	2	5	**15**
Follow my Heart	3	3	4	4	**14**
Embrace Entrepreneurship	5	4	2	5	**16**
Cherish Family and Friends	5	5	5	5	**20**
Explore New Adventures	5	4	4	4	**17**

My BPI Comparison Chart

Big Picture Issue (BPI)	Importance	Feasibility	Resources	Leverage	Total

Choosing a Strategy Exercise
Part 2: Identifying My Top BPIs

Add up your scores. Which BPIs have emerged as your top 3-5? How relevant are these areas to the fulfillment of your mission and overarching vision? Will they help you to live out your core values and brand promise? If addressed, will they help you to move forward in other areas? What is the return on investment for the amount of effort required to see change in these areas? Do a gut check. Do you agree that these should be the highest priority areas for you to tackle over your planning horizon? If not, reorder your list until you are satisfied that you have your top 3-5 issues. When you are content, write your top 3-5 BPIs in priority order in the space provided.

Freeman's Top 5 BPIs

1. Cherish Family & Friends
2. Enjoy the Journey*
3. Focus More on Freeman*
4. Explore New Adventures
5. Embrace Entrepreneurship
6. Improve Health & Physical Fitness

*Freeman decided to combine BPI #2 and BPI #3, so he has five BPIs.

My Top 3-5 BPIs

Getting from Here to There

Have you ever used an online service to get driving directions? One of my favorites is Rand McNally. You type in the address you are leaving from first. Then, you fill in the "to" field with the address of your destination. You press enter and..voila! Directions pop up, along with the distance between your starting and ending points, and an estimated travel time.

Now that your BPIs are selected and prioritized, you are going to write "from-to" statements for each of them. A "from-to" statement helps to define the distance you must cross to get where you would like to go. They are useful when articulating the progress you hope to make with your BPIs.

The "from" component of the statement identifies where you currently are in relationship to your BPI. The "to" field articulates your target; that is, where you would like to be by the closing date of your planning horizon.

Choosing a Strategy Exercise
Part 3: "From-To" Statements

You will use the "be, do, have, give" formula that you used to create your vision statements as the framework for your BPI "from-to" statements. Work on one BPI at a time, using the worksheet that follows.

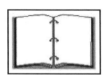 When you have a "from-to" statement for each of your BPIs, transfer all of the statements onto the BPI Life Plan Page provided.

 Or, if you prefer, visit our website at *www.trailblazers-inc. com* and download the BPI Life Plan Page there.

CHAPTER THREE

Freeman's Sample "From-To" Worksheet

BPI Category: Enjoy the Journey/Focus More on Freeman	
Now (at this present moment)	**Then** (at the end of your planning horizon)
Be – Who are you right now as it relates to this BPI? -a single father who focuses almost exclusively on raising his children	Be – Who do you want to become as it relates to this BPI? -the father of three young adults who has more time and freedom to focus on himself and what he enjoys
Do -What are you currently doing related to this BPI? -coming straight home on weeknights and staying in most weekends to run errands and do chores around the house	*Do – What do you hope to accomplish as it relates to this BPI?* -getting out to enjoy myself more, especially on the weekends
Have – What do you currently have related to this BPI? -a somewhat routine, mundane social life	*Have – What do you hope to have as it relates to this BPI?* -an exciting, fulfilling social life
Give: What are you currently giving or sharing when it comes to this BPI? -a fairly boring, predictable me	*Give: What do you hope to give or share when it comes to this BPI?* -a more adventurous, fun-loving me

Using the information above, draft your "from-to" statement for the aforementioned BPI here.

In an effort to enjoy the journey and focus more on myself, I will move from being a single father who focuses almost exclusively on raising his children to being the father of three young adults who has more time and freedom to focus on himself and what he enjoys; I will move from coming straight home on weeknights and staying in most weekends to do chores around the house to getting out to enjoy myself more, especially on weekends; from a somewhat routine, mundane social life to an exciting, fulfilling social life; and from a fairly boring, predictable me to a more adventurous, fun-loving me.

Your "From-To" Worksheet

BPI Category:	
Now (at this present moment)	**Then** (at the end of your planning horizon)
Be – Who are you right now as it relates to this BPI?	*Be – Who do you want to become as it relates to this BPI?*
Do -What are you currently doing related to this BPI?	*Do – What do you hope to accomplish as it relates to this BPI?*
Have – What do you currently have related to this BPI?	*Have – What do you hope to have as it relates to this BPI?*
Give: What are you currently giving or sharing when it comes to this BPI?	*Give: What do you hope to give or share when it comes to this BPI?*

Using the information from your worksheet, draft your "from-to" statement for the aforementioned BPI here:

My " From-To " Statement

My "From-To" Statements

Minding the Gap

I grew up in Philadelphia, so I am accustomed to catching the subway. Each time the door opens at a stop, there is a recorded message that blasts through the station reminding riders to "mind the gap." The gap referred to here is the space between the train and the platform. The warning comes so that passengers getting off the train won't mistakenly step into the gap and get hurt.

There is a gap between "from" (where you are now) and "to" (where you want to go). Failure to mind the gap could harm your future. In the next exercise, you will use the S.W.O.T. Matrix to "mind" the gaps that you are facing and strategize ways to safely eliminate them. A S.W.O.T. Matrix is a framework for analyzing your strengths and weaknesses, as well as the opportunities and threats that you face. I also find it to be a useful tool for exploring successes and failures.

Choosing a Strategy Exercise Part 4: S.W.O.T. Analysis

Using the questions provided, reflect upon your strengths/successes, weaknesses/failures, opportunities and threats in each of the top 3-5 BPIs that you have identified. Be as specific as possible, answering the questions as thoroughly as you can. Don't forget to list your habits, attitudes, and skills.

Please be honest and thoughtful in your responses, and try not to leave any of the boxes blank. The answers you provide are critically important. This information will be used to craft strategies as you launch ME, Inc.

S.W.O.T. Analysis:
Questions to Consider

- What do you do well as it relates to this particular area?

- What are the unique resources you can draw on related to this area?

- What do others see as your strengths related to this area?

- What past successes or victories have you had in this area?

- What positive family traditions or history exists in this area?

- What can be improved in this particular area?

- Where do you lack resources or skills in this particular area?

- What do others see as your particular weaknesses in this area?

- What past failures or challenges have you had in this area?

- What negative family traditions or family history exists relative to this area?

- What opportunites are open to you right now in this particular area?

- What trends could you take advantage of relative to this area?

- What threats do your weaknesses in this particular area expose you to?

- What trends related to this area could harm you?

Sample S.W.O.T. Matrix from Liberty

Strengths
- Bachelor's Degree
- Strong interpersonal skills
- Good growth potential at work
- Knowledgeable in my field
- Family of diligent workers with excellent work ethic

Weaknesses
- Need Master's Degree for promotion
- Low self-esteem
- Lay off reinforced insecurities
- Family tradition of low expectations

BPI: Career & Professional Development

Opportunities
- Tuition reimbursement
- Management Training Program at work
- Current trend of promoting from within the company

Threats
- Low self-esteem prevents me from asserting myself and exuding confidence
- Competitive colleagues pursuing same positions

My S.W.O.T. Matrix

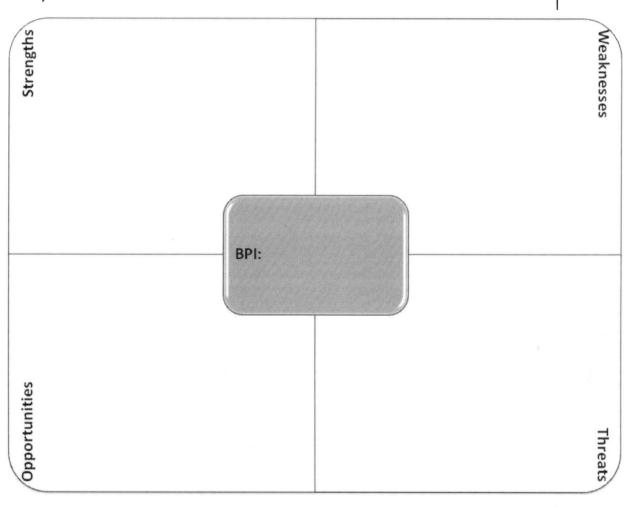

Turning Stumbling Blocks into Stepping Stones

Your next job is to brainstorm the strategic options available to you for closing the gap. You have identified your strengths and weaknesses, your past successes and failures, and the opportunities and threats that exist. Now, you will examine how to capitalize on your strengths and take advantage of opportunities while, at the same time, minimizing the impact of your weaknesses and protecting yourself against threats.

Look at it this way, there are basically stepping stones and stumbling blocks that lie along the path from "here" to "there." Traditionally, stepping stones were placed across a shallow river or stream to form a "bridge." In strategic planning, stepping stones are strengths or opportunities that provide a means of progress or advancement towards your goal. A stumbling block is any obstacle or impediment that stands in the way of you getting to your desired destination. It is a hindrance or obstacle resulting from a weaknesses or threat. You want to create as many stepping stones as possible while eliminating all of the stumbling blocks that you can.

Choosing a Strategy Exercise
Part 5: Weighing My Options

The following exercise will help you devise strategies to build stepping stones and get rid of stumbling blocks. It is called a T.O.W.S. Analysis. The T.O.W.S. Analysis is a relatively simple tool for generating strategic options.

You will do a separate T.O.W.S. Analysis for each BPI. Begin by filling in the boxes around the outer edges with the strengths, weaknesses, opportunities and threats that you identified in your S.W.O.T. Matrix. Then, begin to fill in the boxes in the center, as follows:

- **Strengths and Past Successes/Opportunities** (S/O) – Which strengths most need to be maintained or built upon? Which opportunities should be prioritized, captured or optimized? How can you use your past successes to help you do so? How can you leverage strengths and past successes to take advantage of opportunities and create stepping stones to the future?

- **Strengths and Past Successes/Threats** (S/T) – How can you take advantage of your strengths and past successes to avoid real and potential threats? How do you use your strengths and past successes to eliminate or reduce the possibility of threats becoming stumbling blocks?

- **Weaknesses/Opportunities** (W/O) – How can you use your opportunities to overcome the weaknesses that you are experiencing?

- **Weaknesses/Threats** (W/T) – Which weaknesses most need to be remedied, changed or stopped? Which threats will you focus upon countering or minimizing and managing? What can you learn from your past failures to create greater success and minimize threats in the future? How can you minimize your weaknesses and avoid threats to prevent them from becoming stumbling blocks?

Review all of the possibilities that you have come up with. Identify the top three strategies that you would like to pursue for each BPI. These strategies will remain consistent and help keep you focused over your planning horizon, so they should be broad and sweeping. For example, a strategy is to "further my education," not to "register for classes."

CHAPTER THREE

Liberty's T.O.W.S. MATRIX for _Career_

(Big Picture Issue)

	Opportunities (O) 1. Tuition reimbursement 2. Management Training at work 3. Promotion within company	Threats (T) 1.Lack of confidence 2.Lack of assertiveness 3.Competitive colleagues
Strengths/Successes (S) 1. Bachelor's Degree 2. Interpersonal Skills 3. Growth potential at work 4. Family of hard workers with excellent work ethic	S/O: Strategies that **use strengths and past successes** to **leverage opportunities** and **create stepping stones** 1.Use tuition reimbursement to finish Master's Degree 2.Network using my people skills 3.Attend Mgmt Training seminars to carve a path to advancement 4.Work hard/show diligence in current position to gain leverage for promotion	S/T: Strategies that **use strengths and past successes** to **eliminate** or **minimize threats that are potential stumbling blocks** 1. Draw confidence from high GPA in undergrad studies 2. Use strong people skills as leverage to competition 3. Use excellent work ethic to set myself apart from colleagues
Weaknesses (W) 1. Need master's degree to advance 2. Low self esteem 3. Lay off reinforced insecurities 4. Family tradition of low expectations	W/O: Strategies that **overcome** or **minimize weaknesses** and **past failures** by taking **advantage of opportunities.** 1. Use tuition reimbursement to finish Master's Degree 2. Read books, use prayer, mgmt training and other resources to overcome self-esteem issues, insecurities, and low expectations	W/T: Strategies that **minimize weaknesses** or **past failures** to **prevent threats from becoming stumbling blocks.** Overcome insecurities, break traditions of low expectations and increase confidence through daily prayer and reciting of affirmations, and by attending women's support group meetings at church Complete Life Plan and use as a tool to get off my running wheel

The top three strategies that I would like to pursue in this BPI are: Complete my Master's Degree; take Management Training Certification seminars at work; and make a concentrated effort to overcome insecurities.

My T.O.W.S. MATRIX for _____

(List BPI)

	Opportunities (O) 1. 2. 3. 4.	Threats (T) 1. 2. 3. 4.
Strengths/Successes (S) 1. 2. 3. 4.	S/O: Strategies that **use strengths and past successes to leverage opportunities** and **create stepping stones**	S/T: Strategies that **use strengths and past successes to eliminate** or **minimize threats that are potential stumbling blocks**
Weaknesses (W) 1. 2. 3. 4.	W/O: Strategies that **overcome** or **minimize weaknesses** and **past failures** by taking **advantage of opportunities**	W/T: Strategies that **minimize weaknesses** or **past failures** to **prevent threats from becoming stumbling blocks**

The top three strategies that I would like to pursue in this BPI are:

-
-
-

Conclusion

In this chapter, you identified 3-5 BPIs, as well as some tangible strategies for how to move forward in each area. In the next chapter, we will break each strategy down into goals and action steps.

www.trailblazers-inc.com

Countdown to Launch

Chart your progress by shading in the
steps that you have completed.

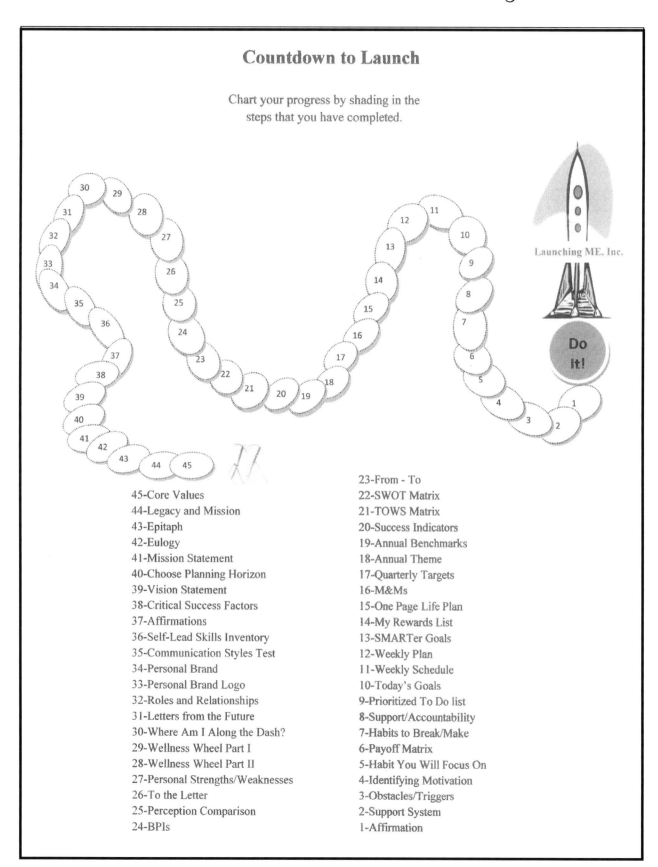

Launching ME, Inc.

Do It!

45-Core Values
44-Legacy and Mission
43-Epitaph
42-Eulogy
41-Mission Statement
40-Choose Planning Horizon
39-Vision Statement
38-Critical Success Factors
37-Affirmations
36-Self-Lead Skills Inventory
35-Communication Styles Test
34-Personal Brand
33-Personal Brand Logo
32-Roles and Relationships
31-Letters from the Future
30-Where Am I Along the Dash?
29-Wellness Wheel Part I
28-Wellness Wheel Part II
27-Personal Strengths/Weaknesses
26-To the Letter
25-Perception Comparison
24-BPIs

23-From - To
22-SWOT Matrix
21-TOWS Matrix
20-Success Indicators
19-Annual Benchmarks
18-Annual Theme
17-Quarterly Targets
16-M&Ms
15-One Page Life Plan
14-My Rewards List
13-SMARTer Goals
12-Weekly Plan
11-Weekly Schedule
10-Today's Goals
9-Prioritized To Do list
8-Support/Accountability
7-Habits to Break/Make
6-Payoff Matrix
5-Habit You Will Focus On
4-Identifying Motivation
3-Obstacles/Triggers
2-Support System
1-Affirmation

CHAPTER 4 **ESTABLISH GOALS & PRIORITIES**

DEVELOPING A PLAN TO MAKE IT HAPPEN

"Man is a goal-seeking animal. His life only has meaning if he is reaching out and striving for his goals."
-Aristotle

Establishing Priorities

By now, you have some idea of how you would like to move forward with the launch of Me, Inc. You have identified your starting point, selected your destination, and explored the various routes that are available. Now, it's time to chart your course.

Drivers who sit staring all day long at a roadmap or GPS pondering their options won't get very far. If they are going to reach their intended destination, they must select a route and start driving.

Choosing which path to take is difficult at times. Each road may be appealing for a different reason. Sometimes, those reasons even conflict with one another and you find yourself faced with competing values. For example, you may value relaxing and enjoying the scenery on a country road. At the same time, being punctual is important to you. If you can't take the country road and be on time, which one do you pick? You must decide which value is more important to you. In essence, you must prioritize.

In this chapter, you will actually draw your road map and pack for the trip. You will decide where to start and determine how to proceed from there. You will anticipate potential obstacles and ways to bypass and overcome them. You will establish which resources are needed to complete your journey and in what quantity. In essence, you will design turn-by-turn directions that are similar to the ones a GPS spits out when you are driving. Of course, there may be a need to "recalculate" along the way; however, this is an opportunity to narrow your focus and maximize your chances for successfully reaching your destination.

Climbing the Ladder

Your journey towards your long-term goals parallels the experience of climbing a ladder. Each and every step you take moves you a little closer to your goal. In the case of your Strategic Life Plan, the smaller steps—your weekly goals and daily tasks—are on the bottom rungs of the ladder. Success on the bottom of the ladder brings you closer to the top of the ladder where you will find the larger steps—your mission, vision, core values and long-term goals.

I can remember climbing up the steps that led to the top of the sliding board as a child. I was so intent on getting to the top as quickly as I could that once I started climbing—I never looked back. My eyes were fixed on the top of those stairs that I knew led to the ride of a lifetime. Often, when I reached the top, my heart would begin to pound—not just in anticipation of going down the slide—but in amazement of how far I had actually climbed.

This chapter will help you to discover the steps needed to get to the top of the ladder. In and of themselves, those steps are not very exciting. You will break your multi-year vision down into an annual plan; you will divide your yearly plan into quarterly targets; you will identify monthly milestones and markers for each quarter; you will translate your monthly milestones and markers into weekly action plans; and, finally, you will use your weekly action plan to develop a daily to-do list.

Essentially, as you plan, you will start at the top of the ladder and work your way down until your vision, mission and core values have been translated into small, practical steps that can be taken on a daily basis. Then, once you have successfully identified all of the rungs on the ladder, you will begin the implementation phase of your plan (explained in Chapter 5) by climbing your way back to the top of the ladder—step-by-step. (See figure 2.)

Sounds pretty mundane, right? Climbing the steps to the sliding board wasn't nearly as exciting as going down the slide, but, if I wanted to experience the exhilaration of coming down that slide with my arms raised in victory, I had to climb the stairs.

There just wasn't any way around it. Similarly, if you will focus on getting to the top of the ladder one step at a time, then you will discover a great life awaits you on the other side!

Remember, your mission and vision are not achievable in one simple step – you must take a journey to get there. If there is a disconnect between your vision for the future and your day-to-day tasks, then you will find yourself back on the running wheel—going about your life haphazardly and failing to make progress toward your long-term goals. All of the hard work that you have done in planning so far will become utterly useless if there is no grounding in your day-to-day realities.

Prepare to make some tough decisions in order to align what you do each day with your long-term goals and values. The exercises that follow will help you to break your vision of the future into daily actions – rungs on the ladder that will eventually lead to the achievement of your long-term priorities. You are about to embark upon Step 4 of the F.R.E.E.D. Coaching Model as you Establish Goals and Priorities.

CHAPTER FOUR

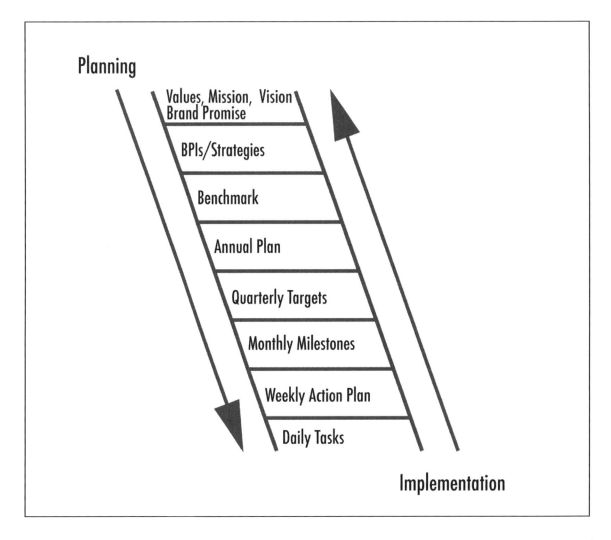

Identifying Benchmarks for Success

In previous chapters, you laid a foundation for success. You established your mission, vision and core values. You also identified your most crucial BPIs and devised strategies for getting you from where you are to where you desire to go. The next step is to establish benchmarks.

Benchmarks are guidelines against which you measure or judge your progress. They set the standard for achievement. These signposts tell us if we are successful, if we are moving towards or away from our goal, and how to adjust ourselves if we are off course.

Indicators are used to develop benchmarks. An indicator is a characteristic that helps assess the extent to which a strategy is working. It is subject to measurement (directly or indirectly).

There are two different types of indicators. The first type is an affective or subjective indicator. These indicators reflect changes in your feelings, opinions or attitudes. Normally, they are measured by investigating how you feel about something or view something. They include things such as how much you enjoy an activity or appreciate a relationship. Declarative or objective indicators are the second type. They are measured by dates, numbers or some other quantitative criteria. They include the number of pounds you would like to lose, the amount of salary you intend to make, the number of hours you plan to work out, etc. Declarative or objective indicators are monitored by collecting, reporting and evaluating numbers. Both types of indicators are valid and applicable for different types of benchmarks.

Your next activity is to establish benchmarks for the strategies you identified in Chapter 3, so that you will be able to measure your progress.

Creating Benchmarks Exercise Part 1: Identifying Success Indicators

Transfer the BPIs and corresponding strategies that you selected for each of them into the first column of the table that is provided on page 171. Next, using your "from-to" statements as a frame of reference, decide which indicators you will use to measure each strategy. Be specific. A list of potential indicators follows:

Sample Indicators:

Fitness and Physical Health
- Number of pounds lost
- Amount of exercise
- Amount of water drank
- Miles walked
- Amount of sleep

Career & Professional Development
- Performance level
- Amount of compensation

- Job rank
- Level of satisfaction
- Number of people served or helped

Wealth & Finances
- Amount saved in various accounts
- Dollars donated to a particular cause
- Frequency of adhering to budget
- Credit rating
- Amount of debt/income-to-debt ratio

Spirituality
- Amount of time spent reflecting or meditating
- Frequency of participation in spiritual gatherings or events
- Comfort or satisfaction level with spiritual life
- Degree of alignment between spiritual beliefs and daily actions
- Degree of faith, optimism or hope as expressed through self talk, attitude or outlook on life

Personal Development and Growth
- Number of formal and informal learning opportunities pursued
- Number of hobbies or amount of time spent on hobbies
- Degree to which you understand yourself and your needs
- Satisfaction level with your personal development and growth
- Level of comfort with risk and/or trying something new

Family & Friends
- Level of fulfillment sensed in a particular relationship
- Amount of time spent with family and friends
- Alignment of actions with personal brand promise
- Level of trust and disclosure achieved in a particular relationship
- Number of phone calls made, birthday cards sent, etc.

Recreation & Fun
- Amount of time spent on recreational and fun activities
- Number of recreational and fun activities enjoyed
- Amount or frequency of social events attended
- Balance between work and personal life as measured by amount of time spent on each, ability to separate the two, etc.
- Frequency of laughter

Physical Environment
- Level of comfort with home environment and furnishings
- Amount of time and steps for planned relocation
- Number of things pursued to beautify home or work environment
- Level of comfort with physical appearance of office environment

Creating Benchmarks Exercise Part 2: Destination

Destination

Figure out where you would like to be at the end of your planning horizon in regards to the indicators that you have chosen. Record that information in last column marked "By the end of my planning horizon, I want to be here…"

Creating Benchmarks Exercise Part 3: Mid-Point

Mid-Point

Decide next where you would like to be at the mid-point between today and the end of your planning horizon. Record those thoughts in the appropriate column.

Creating Benchmarks Part 4: One-Year Mark

One-Year Mark

Finally, record where you would like to be one year from now in the appropriate column.

CHAPTER FOUR

Launching ME, Inc.   Dr. Deidre D. Anderson

Sampling of Freeman's Benchmarks

BIG PICTURE AREA / STRATEGY	Indicators	Year: 2011 One year from now, I want to be here:	Year: 2013 At the mid-way point between now and the end of my planning horizon, I want to be here:	Year: 2015 By the end of my planning horizon, I want to be here:
Cherish family & friends / Build a strong bond w/ grandchildren	time spent with grandchildren; special traditions created	having regular monthly "dates" with each of my grandchildren	getting my grandchildren for quarterly themed weekend getaways at Pop-Pop's house	taking all of my grandchildren on annual cross-country trips
Enjoy the journey/ Focus on Freeman / Revive my social life	time spent at child-free social events; increase in friends	a member of at least two community-based social organizations; attending their social gatherings at least once a quarter	going fishing, golfing, swimming or bowling on a bi-weekly basis; going to parties, the theater and out to dinner with friends at least once a month	throwing social parties for family and newly acquired friends at least quarterly at my home
Explore new adventures / Travel abroad	number of new hobbies; skills learned; number of adventurous trips taken	learning at least a few key words in Spanish; taking a beginner's class for photographers; and doing the "explore photography weekend" at the local museum	doing a five-week trip to California; putting my newfound photography skills to practice	taking a two-week trip for (amateur) photographers to Brazil
Embrace Entrepreneurship / Start my upholstery business	number of steps taken towards planning and opening my new upholstery business	having a full-fledged business plan and bank financing to open up my upholstery business	the upholstery business has been up a running for a year; there is enough to cover expenses and turn a net profit of $50--$75,000 per year	the upholstery business has been up and running for three years and has a profit of no less than $150,000 per year
Improve health & physical fitness / Lose weight and tone up	amount of weight loss; time spent exercising (both cardio and strength)	10 lbs. lighter; member of a local gym; working out no less than 3 times a week	20 lbs. lighter working out 3-5 times weekly on a consistent basis	40 lbs. lighter; working out 5-7 times a week on a consistent basis

My Benchmarks

BIG PICTURE AREA / STRATEGY	Indicators	Year: One year from now, I want to be here:	Year: At the mid-way point between now and the end of my planning horizon, I want to be here:	Year: By the end of my planning horizon, I want to be here:

Finishing Touches

Benchmark Checklist

Y	N	Review your benchmarks and answer the following questions. Do they…
		do a good job of helping you to assess the extent to which a particular strategy is working?
		give you something to look forward to?
		have the proper amount of spacing between them?
		tell you if you are moving towards or away from your goals?
		incorporate appropriate success indicators?
		seem practical?

The Benchmark Life Plan page is also available online at *www.trailblazers-inc.com*.

Ask others for help in establishing benchmarks. No one can tell you exactly what you should do to achieve your goal, but one of the best sources for guidelines is to ask those who have done what you hope to achieve. Are there different ways to reach your goal? Inquire of others and learn from their experience without trying to imitate them.

www.trailblazers-inc.com

Developing an Annual Plan

Congratulations, you have established benchmarks for your entire planning horizon! You are now ready to develop goals and action strategies. Goals and action strategies will be established on an annual basis. For the remainder of the activities in this chapter, you will focus solely on the next 12 months. In light of that, your next assignment is to create a theme for the year.

Building a Ladder to Success Exercise Part 1: Annual Theme

Think about the benchmarks that you have set and the key success indicators that will be used to monitor your progress over the upcoming months. Is there a common theme? What mindset must you have in order to reach or even exceed your targets? If you could choose one focus, feeling or attitude to guide you over the next year, what would it be?

Maybe you need to be bold, compassionate, disciplined, resilient or self-reliant. Perhaps there is a phrase that resonates with you: maximize the moment, embrace the possibilities, enjoy the journey, or have an attitude of gratitude.

Write your theme for the next year in the box provided.

Liberty's Annual Theme

Start to Finish; Conquer to Become

My Annual Theme

Finishing Touches

Annual Theme Checklist

Yes	No	
		Reread your theme out loud.
		Does it motivate you?
		Can you envision reading it aloud on a weekly or daily basis for the next year?
		Does it stir your emotion?

Play around with your theme until it resonates with you.

Find creative ways to keep your theme in front of you. A theme is a fun and unique way to remind you of where to focus your time and energy each year. Use a spiral-bound notebook with blank pages and a sturdy cover to create a flip book of images related to your theme. Take your notebook with you wherever you go or leave it standing open on your desk or dresser. Feeling more creative? Have a contest and invite the children in your family or community to design a poster representing your annual theme. Scan the poster and use it as an image on a t-shirt, screen saver, or mouse pad.

Building a Ladder to Success Exercise
Part 2: Developing Quarterly Targets

Now that you have developed a theme, it's time to break your annual plan down into quarterly targets. You will focus on one BPI at a time, using the quarterly targets planning worksheet in the table provided on page 176. You may use the worksheet provided in the workbook or, if you prefer, visit our website at **trailblazers-inc.com** and download the quarterly targets planning worksheet

there. Start with your most critical BPI. Record the BPI and its "from-to" statement in the appropriate spaces. List the top three strategies that you've identified for that particular BPI. Now you are ready to identify your Quarterly Targets. Begin by recording any relevant one-year benchmarks that you identified earlier in your success indicators chart in the column for fourth quarter targets. Then, add any additional targets that you have for that quarter. Next, record your targets for the third quarter. Follow the same steps for the second and first quarters. When you are finished listing your targets for all four quarters, begin a new worksheet for the next BPI. Repeat the process until you have identified quarterly targets for all of your BPIs.

 *Sampling of Freeman's Quarterly Targets*

Planning Worksheet: Quarterly Targets

BPI: Enjoying the Journey/Taking Care of Freeman

From-to-Statement: *In an effort to enjoy the journey and focus more on myself, I will move from being a single father who focuses almost exclusively on raising his children to being the father of three young adults who has more time and freedom to focus on himself and what he enjoys; I will move from coming straight home on weeknights and staying in most weekends to do chores around the house to getting out to enjoy myself more, especially on weekends; from a somewhat routine, mundane social life to an exciting, fulfilling social life; and from a fairly boring, predictable me to a more adventurous, fun-loving me.*

Strategy	Targets: Quarter 1 (in 3 months)	Targets: Quarter 2 (in six months)	Targets: Quarter 3 (in 9 months)	Targets: Quarter 4 (in 12 months)
Revive my social life	Investigate local community organizations and find one to join	Go to a concert	Go to at least one party or cabaret	Host a holiday party at my place
Begin enjoying sports again	Go skiing Get season tickets for the local college football team	Go bike riding at the local park	Join a summer bowling league	Go to at least one Knicks game
Travel to places I desire to visit	Do a day trip to Lancaster	Take a week-long trip to visit my childhood buddy in California	Go on a weekend cruise to the Bahamas	Go with the church on their New York City trip to enjoy shopping, dinner and a show

My Quarterly Targets

Quarterly Targets Planning Worksheet				
BPI:				
From-To Statement:				
Strategy	Targets: Quarter 1	Targets: Quarter 2	Targets: Quarter 3	Targets: Quarter 4

Finishing Touches

Quarterly Targets Checklist

Y	N	Review your quarterly targets and answer the following questions. Do your quarterly targets…
		give you something to look forward to?
		make your goals for the year seem more real or tangible?
		represent a balanced mix of BPIs and/or Key Life Areas?
		provide a sense of urgency and motivation for working towards your annual goals?

Overlap your quarterly targets. Planning ahead is one important element in achieving your goals. Use the goals of one quarter to make it easier to execute goals in the next. Also, keep in mind that you have seasons overlapping your quarters. You have holidays, birthdays and other special occasions. Work your goals around these things. Remember that your life is the reality upon which you base your goals.

M&Ms, Anyone?

Milestones and markers (M&Ms) are significant events, projects or accomplishments that indicate your progress towards achieving your quarterly targets. It is important to identify monthly M&Ms so that you can determine whether or not you are on course or perhaps need to make mid-course corrections. My recommendation is that you develop M&Ms for the upcoming quarter instead of the entire year; I believe it is more effective to complete your M&Ms one quarter at a time and create new ones at the end of each quarter.

CHAPTER FOUR

Building a Ladder to Success Exercise Part 3: Monthly Milestones and Markers

Go back to your Quarterly Targets Planning Worksheets. Highlight all of the targets you identified for three months from now. Then, put an asterisk next to the highlighted targets that would bring you the greatest sense of accomplishment and satisfaction.

Using the Monthly Milestones Planning Worksheet provided, list the major milestones that you would like to accomplish in each of the next few months.

Sampling of Freeman's Monthly Milestones

Month 1:

My milestones for this month:
- *Collect samples of different business plans*
- *Begin walking at the local track again*
- *Research the names of local community organizations of interest*

Month 2:

My milestones for this month:
- *Do research on the upholstery business*
- *Research different fitness centers in the area*
- *Send away for brochures and search the web on local community organizations of interest; talk to current club members*

Month 3:

My milestones for this month:
- Draft a business plan
- Join a fitness center/sign up with a trainer
- Complete my research on community organizations/begin the selection and application process

My Monthly Milestones

Month 1:
My milestones for this month:

-
-
-

Month 2:
My milestones for this month:

-
-
-

Month 3:
My milestones for this month:

-
-
-

Finishing Touches

Monthly Milestones & Markers Checklist

Y	N	Review your monthly milestones and markers. Do they…
		represent projects, events or accomplishments that can reasonably be achieved in a one-month period?
		lead toward the achievement of your quarterly targets?
		give you a reason to celebrate if they are achieved?

The M & M's Life Plan page is also available online at *www.trailblazers-inc.com.*

Actively use your M&Ms to track progress toward your quarterly targets. Use your M&Ms to determine whether or not you are on track to meet your quarterly targets. The progress you make toward your M&Ms helps verify the need for mid-course corrections. If you achieve a milestone early, it may be possible to add additional targets to your quarterly plan or to devote more time and attention to another target that was previously identified. If you're late in reaching a milestone, the overall schedule may need to be adjusted.

www.trailblazers-inc.com

A Bird's Eye View

Congratulations!

You have taken all of the necessary steps to break your multi-year vision into specific aspirations for the upcoming year. You have selected your BPIs and identified benchmarks for them, decided upon an annual theme, developed quarterly targets, and selected monthly milestones and markers. Each of these elements builds on the next to create a big picture outline – the global context you will use to cascade your broader goals down so that they become a part of your weekly plan and daily schedule.

The next exercise that you will complete provides a critical link for ensuring that your day-to-day tasks will lead to the fulfillment of your long-term vision and mission. You will develop a One Page Life Plan. Your One Page Life Plan offers a bird's eye view of what you must accomplish over the next 12 months. It provides a brief summary of the most significant elements of your Strategic Life Plan at a glance.

Your One Page Life Plan will become a well-loved, familiar companion. You will use it on a weekly basis to help monitor your progress and develop your goals. It includes the following elements:

- Mission Statement
- Vision Statement
- Core Values
- Key Roles
- Brand Promise
- Critical Success Factors for Life Divisions
- BPIs
- Quarterly Targets
- Monthly Milestones & Markers

CHAPTER FOUR

Building a Ladder to Success Exercise
Part 4: One Page Life Plan

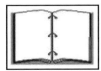

Completing your One Page Life Plan is easy. A template follows. Since you already have all of the necessary items, simply fill in the blanks with the appropriate information. You may use the worksheet provided in this workbook or visit our website at *www.trailblazers-inc.com* to download the One Page Life Plan template.

When you have completed your One Page Life Plan, take a moment to place it your Strategic Life Plan Binder.

www.trailblazers-inc.com

Dr. Deidre D. Anderson

Launching ME, Inc.

Freeman's One-Page Life Plan

This Year's Theme: ***Enjoying the Journey***

Vision Statement for 2015: *I am 50 years old. I am a wonderful father & grandfather; a loving, loyal friend; an entrepreneur; a devoted spouse (or companion); & an active, contributing member of the community. I am spending lots of time with my grandchildren, growing my upholstery business, & building a relationship with that someone special. I have a strong, happy family, a mortgage-free home, a tuition account for my grandchildren, & a loving spouse (or companion) in my life. I am giving my time as a mentor, unconditional love & quality time to my family & friends, & excellent service to my customers.*

Mission Statement: *My mission is to treasure more than anything family, love & perseverance, because these three values hold the key to success & fulfillment for me. Every day, I will live my life in a manner that demonstrates the power to love, the willingness to forgive, & the courage to persist.*

Core Values: *Family, Perseverance, Love*

Key Roles: *Father, Grandfather, Sibling, Friend, Entrepreneur*

Brand Promise: *I help people to find solutions, persist, & remain calm in challenging situations. My level-headedness, loyalty & consistency inspire a sense of peace, security & confidence. I have high standards & deliver with quality & distinction every time.*

Critical Success Factors for Life Divisions:

Physical: *amount of weight loss; time spent exercising (both cardio & strength)*

Financial: *reduction in amount of debt; amount saved for retirement & my grands' tuition account*

Spiritual: *frequency of church attendance & amount of participation; time spent in personal meditation*

Social: *time spent at parties & child-free social events, increase in dating*

Career: *steps taken towards the start of my upholstery business; preparedness to launch the business at year's end*

Friends/Family: *time spent with grandchildren; quality of special traditions created; increase in amount of friends*

Personal Growth: *number of new skills learned*

Fun: *number & quality of trips taken, time spent on hobbies& relaxation; number of parties attended*

BPIs	Quarterly Targets			
	1ˢᵗ Quarter	**2nd Quarter**	**3ʳᵈ Quarter**	**4th Quarter**
Cherish Family & Friends	call my grands once or twice a week	visit my grands or babysit them bi-weekly	take my grands to a movie or museum every other month	do monthly "dates" w/grands; take grands on church trip to NYC
Enjoy the Journey & Focus More on Freeman	complete research on community orgs. that I'm interested in joining; get season tickets; go skiing	join one community organization; attend quarterly meeting; go to a concert; visit childhood friend in CA	join a second community organization; go to a party or cabaret; join a bowling league	host a holiday party at my place; attend end-of-year mtgs. for comm. orgs.; go to a Knicks game; cruise
Explore New Adventures	buy a Spanish-English dictionary;	explore beginner's photography classes & research cameras	save enough to take photography class & buy a camera; purchase CDs on beginner's Spanish	learn at least 50 Spanish words or phrases; take a photography class
Embrace Entrepreneurship	take a class on business planning; research small business loans	price equipment; research financing options	complete business plan draft; work on marketing materials	purchase equipment; begin advertising for business; finish full-fledged business plan & bank financing for upholstery business
Health & Physical Fitness	join the local YMCA; sign up for a personal trainer;	lose at least 5 pounds; work out at least two times a week; go bike riding	maintain weight loss; work out 2-3 times/wk; strive to lose 5 more lbs	lose 10 lbs.; work out no less than 3 times a week

Monthly Milestones & Measures

Jan.: *call grands weekly; gather brochures on comm. orgs; join the Y; sign up for personal trainer; get Span.-Eng. dictionary*	**Apr.** *visit w/ grands; join comm.. org.; research cameras & photography classes; work out*	**July**: *take amusement park trip; work out; join 2nd comm. org.; sign up for summer bowling league; go to Jen's cookout*	**Oct.**: *take grands to science museum; do weekend cruise; finish final biz plan; finalize biz financing; work out*
Feb. *call grands weekly; read through brochures; take biz plan class*	**May**: *visit w/grands; trip to CA/concert in LA/bike riding on Venice Beach; work out*	**Aug.**: *buy camera & sign up for photography class; plan farm trip w/grands; work out; apply for biz financing*	**Nov.**: *attend grandparents' day at my grands' school; go to Knicks game take photography class; work out; purchase equipment for biz*
Mar. *call grands weekly; select 1 comm. org. to join; go on ski trip; research biz loans*	**June**: *visit w/ grands; plan July trip to the amusement park; work out; complete biz plan draft*	**Sept.** *take trip to local farm with grands; work out; purchase Spanish CDs; purchase equipment; start working on advertising plan*	**Dec.** *take grands on trip to NYC; host a holiday party at my place; work out; attend end of year mtg.; advertise grand opening specials*

One Page Life Plan

This Year's Theme:

Vision Statement for 20____:	**Critical Success Factors for Life Divisions:**
Mission Statement:	Physical:
	Financial:
Core Values:	Spiritual:
	Social:
	Career:
Key Roles:	Friends/Family:
	Personal Growth:
Brand Promise:	Fun:

BPIs	Quarterly Targets			
	1st Quarter	2nd Quarter	3rd Quarter	4th Quarter

Monthly Milestones & Measures

Jan.	Apr.	July	Oct.
Feb.	May	Aug.	Nov.
Mar.	June	Sept.	Dec.

Celebrating ME

I absolutely believe in rewarding myself for achieving goals! Recently, I took two fabulous trips to celebrate major accomplishments in my life: a girlfriends' getaway with two of my dearest friends to Sedona, Arizona as a graduation gift to myself when I completed my doctoral studies and a cruise with 30 of my closest family and friends to mark my 40th birthday. I don't wait for major life events, however, to commemorate my progress. I have learned to celebrate the small daily accomplishments with things like a walk in the park, a trip to the sauna at my local gym, or a tall cup of vanilla Chai latte.

We can so easily neglect the importance of acknowledging and celebrating the small victories we experience in life. When I'm tempted to give up, I often stop and remind myself of the small victories I've had. One way to keep those small victories in the forefront of your mind is to pause and celebrate. Little celebrations will help encourage you to continue moving forward until you have the experience and ability to achieve greater things.

Building a Ladder to Success Exercise Part 5: Rewards

In this exercise, you will brainstorm a list of rewards – large and small – that you will use to celebrate victories and alleviate stress in your new role as the CEO of ME, Inc. You will brainstorm three types of rewards:

- Stress Busters
- Time-to-Time Treats
- Rare Rewards

Stress Busters are small treats or quick activities that you can do in 30 minutes or less. They are free or nominal in cost and include such things as taking a walk in the park or treating yourself to a cup of tea. *Time-to-Time Treats* or Triple Ts, as I affectionately call them, are medium-sized rewards that you occasionally enjoy. Whereas Stress Busters are usually spontaneous and spur-of-the-moment, you generally plan for Triple Ts because they require a greater investment of money and time. Triple Ts are things like spending the day at the spa or going on a weekend trip. Finally, there are *Rare Rewards*. These are the super-sized indulgences that you lavish upon yourself for significant achievements or special occasions. What are some of the fun things you want to do before you die? Where are some of the places that you are hoping to visit? Include them all on your Rare Rewards List.

Have fun with this activity. It's important to remember that different things motivate different people. Although I have provided examples for you, you must create your own list filled with things that you enjoy. Be creative. You will use this list later as you develop your goals.

Liberty's Rewards List

Stress Busters (bite-sized)	Time-to-Time Treats (medium-sized)	Rare Rewards (super-sized)
Put candles around the tub and take a bubble bath	Go to a concert	Buy a new car
Treat myself to a movie	Take an afternoon or full-day off to "do nothing"	Take a Hawaiian vacation
Enjoy my favorite dessert or a cup of tea	Enjoy a day at the spa	Go to a luxurious spa retreat
Go shopping or dine out	Go away for an overnight or weekend retreat	Go on a cruise
Enjoy a hobby or go to the museum	Attend a conference	Buy an item for myself that I've always wanted, but have been too frugal to purchase
Get out of the office and go for a walk	Check into a hotel and spend a day lounging by the pool	Treat myself to dinner at the fanciest restaurant in town
Chat with friends or co-workers	Spend a day at an amusement park	Purchase that diamond tennis bracelet
Get some extra sleep	Buy that outfit I've had my eye on	
Listen to my favorite music CD	Treat myself to a total make-over at the salon	
Laugh uncontrollably	Attend a sporting event	
Enjoy a manicure		
Get a foot massage		

www.trailblazers-inc.com

My Rewards List

Stress Busters (bite-sized)	Time-to-Time Treats (medium-sized)	Rare Rewards (super-sized)

Finishing Touches

Rewards Checklist

Y	N	Review your rewards worksheets and answer the following questions:
		Does every reward reflect something that I enjoy?
		Do I have a sufficient mix of bite-sized, medium-sized and super-sized rewards?
		Have I included outrageous things that I dream about doing and buying on my super-sized list?
		Am I motivated by the rewards on my list – both big and small?

The Rewards Life Plan page is also available online at *www.trailblazers-inc.com*.

Share your rewards list with family members, friends and co-workers. They may come up with other creative ideas to add. In addition, it may give them further insight into the things you enjoy. Perhaps they will even use the list to inspire gift giving ideas for your birthday, a holiday, or some other special occasion.

SMARTer Goals

Now that you have determined how you are going to celebrate your success, it's time to break your monthly milestones down into SMARTer goals and action plans. You may have heard of the SMART goal setting technique which is very popular with businesses. We are going to use a similar approach – called SMARTer goal setting – which adds a few additional elements.

The acronym is explained below.

S – Specific

A SMARTer goal is specific. It is a well-defined target that gives you clarity, direction and motivation toward what you want. Our minds do not respond well to vague generalities. If your goal is too general, you will find it difficult

www.trailblazers-inc.com

to achieve because your definition of success is unclear. Choose exact terms to describe your goal. Be clear. Be precise. Be specific. This will help to direct your energy and attention toward what needs to be done in order to achieve your desired outcome.

M – Measurable

A SMARTer goal is measurable. When your goal is measurable, it makes it easier to track your progress, determine if you are going in the right direction, and make any necessary adjustments along the way. Developing measurable goals also helps you to stay on track, reach your target dates, and experience the exhilaration of achievement that motivates you to continue moving forward. To determine if your goal is measurable, ask questions such as "How much? How many? How will I know when it is accomplished?"

A – Action-Oriented

A SMARTer goal is action-oriented. Too often, people set goals and stop there. What actions do you need to take in order to fulfill your goal? You will need to develop a step-by-step strategy. Focus on actions you can take that are in your direct control.

R – Realistic and Relevant

A SMARTer goal is realistic and relevant. Goals need to be relevant to you and to your mission, vision and values. In other words, they need to be meaningful and significant. Remind yourself of why you want to achieve this goal and how it will make a difference in your life.

Goals also need to be realistic. You want to stretch yourself, but your goals must be achievable. Again, they should involve things that you can actually do and control.

T – Time Specific

A SMARTer goal is time specific. Goals without deadlines lend themselves to being put off until another day. Always state your goal with a deadline that is specific, rather than relative (i.e. 23rd of March rather than in 4 weeks).

E – Exciting

A SMARTer goal is exciting. Goals need to be something you are excited about and are going to either enjoy doing or enjoy the outcome. If you aren't motivated by your goals, you probably won't achieve them.

CHAPTER FOUR

R – Rewarded

A SMARTer goal is rewarded. It is important to celebrate your progress. Build in rewards and find ways to commemorate significant milestones and achievements. Using the list of rewards that you brainstormed in the last exercise, take time to consider how you will mark each step of your goal achievement. It could be as simple as giving yourself a pat on the back or treating yourself to a movie. The important thing is that you intentionally celebrate!

Building a Ladder to Success Exercise Part 6: Setting Goals

The next step is to use the SMARTer goal setting process to develop goals that will help you to reach the M&Ms that you identified for the upcoming month. Using the worksheet provided, write out one or two SMARTer goals for each M&M.

Or, if you prefer, visit our website at www.trailblazers-inc.com to access the SMARTer goals planning worksheet online.

SMARTer Goal Setting

BPI/Key Life Area: ***Professional Development***
Monthly Milestone: ***Return to school***
Specific Goal to Reach Milestone: ***Get registered and get started in school***
How will the goal be measured? ***It will be measured by whether or not I am successful in getting registered and started by the deadline.***
Relevancy to mission, vision and core values/Reason goal(s) is important to me ***Continuing my education will boost my self-esteem and give me more confidence. It will also increase my advancement opportunities at work. It will qualify me for my ideal job and position me for a significant increase in salary.***

Action Steps required to achieve goal(s):

Week 1	Week 2	Week 3	Week 4
Notify human resources of my intent to enroll ***Complete necessary paperwork to qualify for tuition reimbursement*** ***Search for and apply for scholarships***	***Complete enrollment/registration process at school*** ***Make an appointment with academic advisor to select courses***	***Pay for classes by deadline*** ***Purchase text books and supplies***	***Start classes***

Is it: √ Realistic √ Exciting
Who will support me and/or hold me accountable? ***My Fiancé***, *Carl*
Rewards/How will I celebrate my progress? ***I will reward myself by attending a concert at the end of the semester.***

SPECIFIC – MEASURABLE – ACTION-ORIENTED – REALISTIC
RELEVANT – TIME-SPECIFIC – EXCITING – REWARDING

SMARTer Goal Setting

BPI/Key Life Area
Monthly Milestone

Specific Goal to Reach Milestone

How will the goal be measured?

Relevancy to mission, vision and core values/Reason goal(s) is important to me

Action Steps required to achieve goal(s):			
Week 1	Week 2	Week 3	Week 4

Is it: ❏ Realistic ❏ Exciting
Who will support me and/or hold me accountable?
Rewards/How will I celebrate my progress?

**SPECIFIC – MEASURABLE – ACTION-ORIENTED – REALISTIC
RELEVANT – TIME-SPECIFIC – EXCITING – REWARDING**

Finishing Touches

SMARTer Goals Checklist

Y	N	
		Review your goal worksheets and see if your goals pass the SMARTer goals test:
		Have you included enough details?
		Are your goals measurable?
		Do your goals require specific actions?
		Do your goals stretch you without being unrealistic?
		Are your goals relevant to your monthly milestones and long-term mission and vision?
		Have you tied your goals to a timeline?
		Do your goals excite you?
		Have you identified who will hold you accountable?
		Did you include at least one reward for each goal?

Keep a success log. At the end of each day, take a few minutes to write down all of your successes, even the small ones. Do this in your personal life, as well as your business life. When you need encouragement, take a few minutes to review your success log.

CHAPTER FOUR

www.trailblazers-inc.com

Planning Your Week

In the last exercise, you identified your SMARTer goals for the upcoming month and broke them down into specific action steps to be achieved each week. It's amazing when you think about it!

You started with a vision of yourself 3-5 years in the future that included a glimpse into what you want each of your key life areas to look like. After honestly assessing your current status, you identified the most critical BPIs that must be addressed in order to move you from where you are to where you want to go. You developed specific strategies and benchmarks to measure your progress for each BPI over the next several years.

Then, you turned your attention to look more closely at the upcoming year. You choose an annual theme and examined what you must achieve each quarter to reach your goals over the next 12 months. You broke your quarterly goals down into M&Ms for the next three months and wrote SMARTer goals complete with weekly action steps.

You are just two steps away from funneling your 3-5 year vision into day-to-day action steps. Instead of spinning your wheels every day, you are about to identify tasks that will deliberately move you towards your Ideal Future on a daily basis. Isn't that exciting? Disciplining yourself to consistently plan your week and use a daily task list to achieve your weekly goals are critical steps in permanently moving your life off of the running wheel so that you can start living life on a Purposeful Pathway as the CEO of ME, Inc.

Your next assignment is to develop an action plan for the upcoming week. Planning the next seven days shouldn't be too difficult, because you have already identified the steps you need to take in your SMARTer goals. Go back and highlight the week one goals on each of your SMARTer goal planning worksheets. When you are done, use the instructions that follow to complete the weekly planning worksheets and develop a plan for next week.

 # Building a Ladder to Success
Part 7: Planning Your Week

Planning your week is a two-step process. There is a worksheet to assist you with each step. The first step is to identify your goals and tasks for the upcoming week. The next step is to create a loose schedule for the week.

Begin with the weekly goals planning worksheet. In light of the action steps that you highlighted on your SMARTer goal worksheets, what are the three most critical goals/tasks that you could achieve this week? List those three goals at the top of the worksheet.

Your next step is to record your remaining goals/tasks for the upcoming week. I recommend doing so by BPI or life category to help assure a more balanced approach to planning. Using your weekly goals planning worksheet, record your BPIs/life categories in the first column. Beside each category, list the associated goals/tasks for the week.

Next, you will develop your schedule for the upcoming week. Remember to be flexible when planning your schedule. Although you will be much more purposeful in your day-to-day living, you must leave room for unscheduled events and crises that arise. The idea is to map out your week to ensure that you have allotted time for your appointments and most important tasks. It is not to pigeon-hole yourself into a rigid schedule that sets you up for failure.

With that in mind, jot down all of your appointments and meetings for the upcoming week using the weekly schedule planning worksheet. Your next step is to identify the time slots needed to complete your three most critical goals/tasks for the week. Mark those items down on your schedule along with the amount of time required for each. Finally, list any other tasks that need to be scheduled.

CHAPTER FOUR

Liberty's Weekly Plan

The three most important goals/tasks that I can accomplish this week are:
1. **Contact Human Resources.**
2. **Record and begin reciting affirmations.**
3. **Go to the library and check out a book on self-esteem.**

BPI or Life Division	Goals/Tasks to be Completed This Week	Complete?
Career/ Professional	Contact Human Resources, get details re: requirements for tuition reimbursement.	
	Complete and submit reimbursement paperwork.	
	Sign up for upcoming Management Training Seminars.	
BPI – Overcoming Insecurities	Purchase voice recorder. Record affirmations. Transfer onto computer. Make CDs.	
	Place one copy in car and one in bedroom. Listen and recite at bedtime and on the commute to and from work.	
	Place hard copies of affirmations in purse, on bathroom mirror, in desk drawer at work. Set phone alarm to remind me to recite them.	
Recreation and Fun	Research biking trails within 20 mile radius.	
	Have safety inspection performed on both bikes.	
	Purchase biking supplies: bike rack, back pack, water bottle, biker shorts, lock and chain.	
Personal Development and Growth	Check out a self-esteem book from the library.	
	Read for 30 minutes during lunch break.	
	Designate one of my unused journals as my "Personal Development Journal." Use it to jot down key points from book.	

My Weekly Plan

The three most important goals/tasks that I can accomplish this week are:

1.

2.

3.

BPI or Life Division	Goals/Tasks to be Completed This Week	Complete?

Liberty's Weekly Schedule

Week of: April 4, 2011

Monday (appointments & projects)	Time Required
Prepare comprehensive list of questions and send to Brenda Atkins in HR	45 minutes
Phone conference with Brenda	45 minutes
Library/Self esteem book	1 hour
Emails: David J. and Collin (copy Collin on both emails)	20 minutes

Tuesday (appointments & projects)	Time Required
Call florist and send gift to Mom	30 minutes
Complete paperwork and submit	1.5 hours
Purchase voice recorder on the way home	45 minutes
Read 30 minutes during lunch break	30 minutes

Wednesday (appointments & projects)	Time Required
Call to wish Mom a happy birthday	1 hour
Register for training	30 minutes
Record affirmations and burn to CDs	1.5 hours
Read 30 minutes during lunch break	30 minutes

Thursday (appointments & projects)	Time Required
Go straight home to meet Carl, pull bikes out of garage for Collin	15 minutes
Carl help me search garage for box of journals	15 minutes
Collin inspects bikes/helps us decide on trail	2 hours
Sporting Goods store with Collin and Carl, purchase any items Carl recommends, plus bike rack, water bottle, shorts, lock and chain	1.5 hours
Read 30 minutes during lunch break	30 minutes

Friday (appointments & projects)	Time Required
Supermarket-be sure to pick up special items for trip	1.5 hours
Pack for trip	2 hours

Saturday/Sunday	Time Required
Bike trip and picnic with Carl!	All day
Visit Carl's parents' church service/Sunday dinner at their home	All day

My Weekly Schedule

Week of:

Monday (appointments & projects)	Time Required

Tuesday (appointments & projects)	Time Required

Wednesday (appointments & projects)	Time Required

Thursday (appointments & projects)	Time Required

Friday (appointments & projects)	Time Required

Saturday/Sunday	Time Required

Finishing Touches

Weekly Planning Checklist

Y	N	Review both worksheets and answer the following questions:
		Do you feel like you have a clear picture of what you want to accomplish over the next week?
		Is your schedule realistic?
		Have you allowed room for flexibility and unexpected occurrences?
		Have you scheduled time for self care and stress management?

If you answered "no" to any of the questions on the checklist, go back and adjust your weekly plan accordingly. When you feel satisfied, take a moment to celebrate. You have just completed a critical step in launching ME, Inc. You have broken your dream down into bite-sized weekly pieces. There is just one more step in establishing your goals and priorities—creating a prioritized daily to do list. You will find out how in the next exercise.

The weekly planning worksheet is also available online at *www.trailblazers-inc.com.*

Add Your Key Life Roles as Weekly Planning Categories. Consider adding your life roles, such as wife, mother and friend, to the list of categories that you use to develop your weekly plan. Identifying goals for each of your key roles will help keep you balanced and ensure that you don't neglect your most vital relationships. Remember, goals on your weekly list should be directly tied to your long-range goals. Get in the habit of periodically reviewing your brand promise and letters to the future to assess how you are doing with your relationships.

One Day at a Time

Our day-to-day habits ultimately determine our success or failure in life. You will never realize your dreams until you develop the discipline to work towards them one day at a time. Seconds turn into minutes, minutes turn into hours, hours turn into days, days turn into weeks, weeks turn into months, months turn into years, and, if you don't become deliberate with moving your life forward, the years will begin to pass you by without any tangible progress made towards your vision.

Your daily routine is the key to your success. How do you go about your day? Do you generally have a plan or are you simply meandering from hour-to-hour? Have you assigned blocks of time to work on your most important projects?

I'm not suggesting that you map out how you will spend every second of your day. You will set yourself up for failure if you do that. What I am asking you to do is to be deliberate about how you spend your time. Time is a precious resource. It's not renewable, so you must be intentional about how you use it.

Having a prioritized to do list will increase your productivity and maximize your time. Not only will it free your mind from the distraction of thinking about what to do next, it will serve as a reminder of the tasks that need your attention throughout the day so that you'll be less apt to waste time elsewhere. In fact, properly preparing and using a daily to do list connected to your weekly goals is one of your most powerful weapons in the fight against life on the running wheel. An exercise follows to help you develop a prioritized to do list. We will talk more about how to use the list in chapter 5.

Building a Ladder to Success
Part 8: Prioritized To Do List

Put tomorrow's date at the top of your to do list. Review your weekly plan and schedule. List the most important task that you want to accomplish for the day. This is called your "Today Goal."

After identifying your "Today Goal," list any additional tasks that you plan to complete that day. When you have all of your tasks for the day listed, prioritize them according to importance (how significant they are) and immediacy (when they are due). I use the A-B-C, 1-2-3 method with most of my clients; however, you may use whatever prioritization system you like. If you choose to use the A-B-C, 1-2-3 method, then begin by identifying which tasks are "A" tasks. Tasks with an "A" label are your highest priority tasks. You must do these tasks immediately. Tasks labeled with a "B" are second priority tasks. They are not tasks that must be completed immediately, but you need to get them soon and it would be nice if you could complete them today. "C"s are low priority tasks. These are things that you would like to do; however, they can wait. Once you have prioritized each task as A, B, or C, go back and number them according to priority in each category.

When you are finished prioritizing your tasks, list all of the appointments that you have for the day, along with their time and location. Be sure to indicate any meeting preparation that needs to be done on your part. Finally, note any emails that need to be sent and calls that need to be made. Doing so will give you two advantages: 1) you will be able to "chunk" your emails or calls together so that you can do them all at once, and 2) you will be able to squeeze calls and emails in during "in between times" when you have a few minutes to spare.

Libby's Prioritized To Do List

Today's Date: *Monday, April 4, 2011*
My Today Goal: *Have a successful call with Brenda Atkins*

To Do	Priority	Calls to Be Made:
Prepare for phone meeting with Brenda Atkins, Human Resources Manager/Email her my list of questions to be discussed prior to making the call	A1	*Brenda Atkins, 333-521-7812 Xerox customer service, 333-987-8641*
Search the web for bike trails	B3	
Download paperwork for tuition reimbursement	C1	**Emails to be Sent**
Schedule travel for Paul's trip to California next month	A3	*Brenda Atkins David Johnston Collin Smith Paul White*
Send reminder email to participants in next week's meeting	B1	
Call for service to the copier	A4	
Email David Johnston – ask for recommendations of his favorite bike trails	C3	
Email Collin – remind him to stop by and inspect bikes on Thursday evening	B2	
Stop by library – pick up self-esteem book	A5	
Finish Paul's edits to the report /send it to him for final approval	A2	
Get a smoothie to celebrate finally scheduling and completing the HR call with Brenda	C2	

Daily Appointment List

Time & Place	Appointment	Preparation Needed?
11:15 am Phone Appointment	Brenda Atkins, Human Resources Ext. 2143	Send her a list of questions.

www.trailblazers-inc.com

My Prioritized To Do List

Today's Date:

My Today Goal:

To Do	Priority	Calls to Be Made:
		E-Mails to Be Sent:

Daily Appointment List

Time & Place	Appointment	Preparation Needed?

Finishing Touches

Daily To-Do Checklist

Y	N	Review your to do list and answer the following questions:
		Have I established my most important priorities?
		Does my daily to do list link back to my weekly plan?
		Have I noted my appointments, as well as emails and calls that need to be handled?
		Do I feel that I can reasonably accomplish everything on my list?

Did you answer "no" to any of the questions on the checklist? Make adjustments to your to do list, as necessary.

The daily to do planning worksheet is also available online at *www.trailblazers-inc.com*.

Schedule some fun time on your to do list. Your to do list doesn't have to be a series of mundane duties. Going to the movies or enjoying a walk in the park may not seem as important as some of your other tasks, but such activities are crucial to your mental and emotional health. Incorporating things you enjoy into your to do list not only makes you well-rounded, it enables you to associate your list with positive thoughts and feelings. Think of your list as a source of joy and strength – a lifeline that pulls you from the grip of the running wheel. If you see your list in this light, you'll be less resistant to doing the work required to maintain it.

Conclusion

Congratulations! You have managed to break your dreams down into milestones, goals and daily action steps. Undoubtedly, you are well on your way to turning your dreams into reality. Your plan is nearly complete. You've prepared yourself well. ME, Inc. is almost ready to be unveiled. The only thing left is for you to take the leap. It's time to "Do It"!

Countdown to Launch

Chart your progress by shading in the
steps that you have completed.

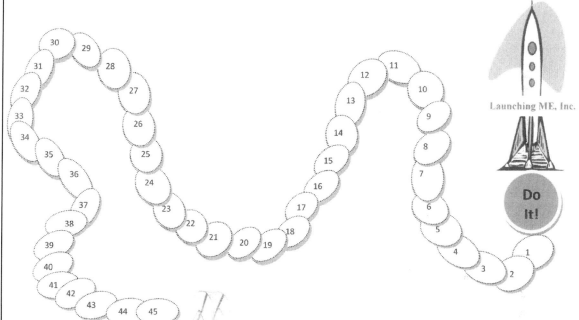

Launching ME, Inc.

Do It!

45-Core Values
44-Legacy and Mission
43-Epitaph
42-Eulogy
41-Mission Statement
40-Choose Planning Horizon
39-Vision Statement
38-Critical Success Factors
37-Affirmations
36-Self-Lead Skills Inventory
35-Communication Styles Test
34-Personal Brand
33-Personal Brand Logo
32-Roles and Relationships
31-Letters from the Future
30-Where Am I Along the Dash?
29-Wellness Wheel Part I
28-Wellness Wheel Part II
27-Personal Strengths/Weaknesses
26-To the Letter
25-Perception Comparison
24-BPIs

23-From - To
22-SWOT Matrix
21-TOWS Matrix
20-Success Indicators
19-Annual Benchmarks
18-Annual Theme
17-Quarterly Targets
16-M&Ms
15-One Page Life Plan
14-My Rewards List
13-SMARTer Goals
12-Weekly Plan
11-Weekly Schedule
10-Today's Goals
9-Prioritized To Do list
8-Support/Accountability
7-Habits to Break/Make
6-Payoff Matrix
5-Habit You Will Focus On
4-Identifying Motivation
3-Obstacles/Triggers
2-Support System
1-Affirmation

CHAPTER 5

TAKE ACTION

"Plans are just good intentions
unless they immediately
degenerate into hard work."
— Peter Drucker

www.trailblazers-inc.com

Breathing Life Into Your Plan

You have spent a significant amount of time preparing for your launch. You've dreamed about your Ideal Future, identified your mission and vision, and developed your brand promise. You've assessed your strengths and weaknesses as well as your past successes and failures, and identified stepping stones and stumbling blocks. You've evaluated the gap between where you are and where you want to go and devised strategies, goals and objectives to get you from here to there. Now, it's time for you to take action. It's time for you to "Do It"—implement your plan and launch ME, Inc.

I've seen far too many strategic planning exercises fail because they ended without effectively achieving implementation. After completing the goal setting process, many people lose sight of the next critical step: implementing their plans so that they become living documents that actually guide their day-to-day decision making and move them towards their Ideal Future.

The fact is that lots of people create beautiful strategic plans. They are glossy and colorful and laid out to perfection with fancy tables and charts. Far too often, however, those plans are written and then ignored. People look at them and say, "Hey, that's nice"… put them away, and no one ever looks at them again. Planning efforts are wasted because the documents sit on a shelf or become lost on a hard drive.

Implementation helps you to construct a process that connects your Strategic Life Plan with your day-to-day appointments and daily to do list. You use your plan to guide you through each day, week, month, quarter and year. In that way, your daily activities, rather than being distractions that keep you from reaching your goals, become stepping stones to achieving them.

Remember, writing your Strategic Life Plan is not the final step in accomplishing the goals outlined in the plan. Without certain essential actions and activities on your part, your plan will simply collect dust. You've worked too hard to allow that to happen.

This final chapter will address six critical activities that are necessary to effectively implement your plan. They are:

1. Monitor, Monitor, Monitor;
2. Make Adjustments;
3. Reach Out for Support;
4. Celebrate;
5. Master Your Day; and
6. Take the Challenge.

We will walk you through each step. Are you ready? Let's "Do It"!

Monitor, Monitor, Monitor!

The first step in successfully implementing your Strategic Life Plan is to keep it before you. You have created two reports as a result of walking through the exercises outlined in this book.

1. **STRATEGIC LIFE PLAN:** This first is a complete Strategic Life Plan comprised of all of your Life Plan Pages. I suggest that you purchase a binder or a folder, so that you may store all of your pages in the same place and access them easily. You will reference your entire Strategic Life Plan during annual and quarterly planning (and any other time you decide it is needed).

2. **ONE PAGE LIFE PLAN:** The other is your One-Page Life Plan. This is your GPS—a document you will use consistently for ongoing planning and communication purposes.

Think about how you use a GPS. You keep your GPS mounted on your windshield. Although it is not "front and center" in your view, you can always see it out of the corner of your eye. It's in your peripheral. Occasionally, you glance at it to make sure you are on the right path. And, when you make a wrong turn, it lets you know and attempts to guide you back on the right path. Like your GPS, you must always keep your plan in your view. It should be regularly monitored, evaluated, and adapted. You must keep your eye on it, so you can consistently assess what is working (and why) and what is not working (and why). By watching your plan, you see where you need to go. Otherwise, it is easy to lose sight of the road to success and become bogged down in day-to-day, mundane tasks.

I suggest you review your One Page Life Plan each week when you sit down to write your weekly goals. That way, you are reminded, not only of your mission and vision, but also of your quarterly targets and monthly milestones. Be sure to link your weekly goals to your monthly milestones. In addition, review your brand promise, critical success factors and BPIs to see if you want to add any additional goals for the week. At the end of the month, you can also use your One Page Life Plan as a reference for updating your monthly milestones, if necessary.

A more formal evaluation, using your complete Strategic Life Plan, should be done on a quarterly and annual basis. At the end of each quarter, take a day to review your progress and adjust your targets for the upcoming quarter. Be sure to consider the following:

- How much progress has been made in reaching your benchmarks?
- What is preventing you from moving forward?

www.trailblazers-inc.com

- What adjustments should be made to your quarterly targets?
- Is there a need to go back and revise your annual plan?

Of course, the most thorough update is done annually. Once a year, I spend a few days away from home for a planning retreat. I generally go through the evaluation process outlined in Chapter 2 and bring the results with me for review. I reflect upon my accomplishments and challenges from the previous year and spend some time meditating and determining my annual theme. I also revise my benchmarks, milestones, goals and action plans for the upcoming year.

Establish routines for each time you plan. Whether it is your annual, quarterly, monthly or weekly review, be sure to look over your vision, mission, core values and brand promise statement. Constantly meditating on these critical guideposts will keep them in the forefront of your mind. When you have tough decisions to make, pull them out and review them. A great habit to cultivate is to ask a series of questions for each and every major decision: "Does this help to further my mission? How will it fit into my vision for the future? Does it reinforce my values and brand promise?"

Remember, strategic life planning is a dynamic process that involves continuously looking at your current situation and plotting your next move. Strategic plans must be flexible and open to revision.

While you must track your progress and hold yourself accountable, keep in mind that there will be unexpected bumps in the road and that you need to forgive yourself if you veer off track. Simply get back on course and begin moving forward in the right direction. Don't continue going down the wrong path. Be willing to make adjustments.

Make Adjustments

Keep in mind that, although writing your Strategic Life Plan is critically important, no part of it is written in stone—not your mission, vision, values, brand promise nor any of the goals or steps. Just as a strategic plan in a business or organization needs to be adjusted occasionally, your Strategic Life Plan will require some changes as you go along. Remember, life intervenes from time to time, requiring modifications in timing, steps, and resources.

It's OK to deviate from your plan. In fact, it is a mistake to think you will never digress or stray away. Your plan is not a set of rules. It is a guideline. While it's helpful to have all the right systems in place to track your progress, acknowledging contingencies and adjusting your actions is a critical part of planning. Your efforts are all for naught if you lack the will and the flexibility

www.trailblazers-inc.com

necessary to make adjustments along the way. Over time, and presented with solid evidence, you can't be afraid to depart from the original plan.

When there's a difference between what you've achieved and your target, you must determine what to do to bring the two in line. Take a look at all of the factors that are keeping you from accomplishing your goal and develop a plan to overcome them. There are several possible options.

1. **Implement Some New Actions** – These actions will help you close the gap between where you are and where you want to be. They will be actions that will impact your benchmarks and move you closer to your target.

2. **Modify What You're Already Doing** – You could do more or less of something that you are already doing. By making changes to something you are already doing, you will help your progress move more quickly towards the target.

3. **Change Your Target** – If the different ways of reaching your target didn't work, you may want to change your target. For example, if your initial goal was to earn an additional $15,000 this year but the economy tanks and you realize that your goal is unrealistic, adjust your plan accordingly.

In addition, because we cannot possibly predict everything that will happen in our future, sometimes we encounter a crisis or life change that causes us to take a detour from our original plan. That's OK. In fact, it is to be expected. Remember Emergency Landing on Running Wheel Row? The Managing Detours worksheet included in the appendix is intended to help you manage life's detours so that you don't get stuck in crisis mode.

Finally, if you find that you just aren't making progress, consider reaching out for additional assistance - hire a coach or tap into the support of loved ones. Don't allow the goals you've worked so hard on to just fade away. Figure out what you need to do to accomplish them and adjust your plan accordingly.

Reach Out for Support

It is very easy to assume that a Strategic Life Plan only needs to be read by the person who wrote it. That is a misperception. An important step in implementing your Strategic Life Plan is to communicate the contents of the plan to the people who will support you in implementing it. Tackling your long-term objectives is not something that you want to do solo. In fact, nothing great is ever accomplished by one person acting alone. Who are the people who can support you in trying to reach your goals? Who are the people who are likely to encourage you as you strive to reach those goals? These are the people with whom you want to sit down, spend some time, and just share what you put together as your goals for the year.

In fact, I encourage everyone implementing a Strategic Life Plan to find an accountability partner. An accountability partner will not only help to encourage you, he or she will also help you to avoid becoming distracted and getting off track. My best friend also happens to be my accountability partner. She comes with me on my annual planning retreat and we review our Strategic Life Plans together. Once a quarter, we also get together to assess our progress for the previous quarter and make the necessary adjustments for the upcoming three months. In addition, we email a weekly report to one another that summarizes our progress for the previous week and lists our goals for the week to come. This process has been invaluable to me! I know I owe much of my progress to the process that my accountability partner and I follow on a consistent basis.

In the space provided, write down the names of all of the people that you will share your Strategic Life Plan with. Then, brainstorm a list of potential accountability partners.

People I will Share My Plan With

Potential Accountability Partners

Celebrate!

Accomplishments of any consequence take time to achieve. Even the most disciplined among us need to be motivated and inspired to achieve long-term goals. It's easy to become tired and cynical when we accomplish a desired result and move on to the next goal without pausing to celebrate. The process can seem like having to solve one problem after another, with no end in sight. Yet, it is a major triumph to actually achieve results. So, acknowledge this – take time to reward yourself!

In Chapter 4, you created a rewards list. Don't let that list go to waste. When you've achieved a goal, take the time to enjoy the satisfaction of having done so. Absorb the implications of the goal achievement, and observe the progress that you've made towards other goals.

If the goal was a significant one, reward yourself appropriately. All of this helps you build the self-confidence you will need to continue forging forward.

After celebrating your accomplishment, review the rest of your goal plans:

- If you achieved the goal too easily, make your next goal more difficult.

- If the goal was especially hard to achieve, make the next goal a little easier.

- If you learned something that would lead you to change other goals, do so.

- If you noticed a deficit in your skills despite achieving the goal, decide whether to set goals to build your skill set.

Master Your Day

Ultimately, our day-to-day habits determine our success or failure in life. You will never realize your dreams until you develop the discipline to work towards them one day at a time. Days turn into weeks, weeks turn into months, months turn into years, and, if you don't become deliberate with moving your life forward, the years will begin to pass you by without any tangible progress made towards your vision. Sounds like life on the running wheel, doesn't it? Thank goodness that is a life that you have left behind.

Your new life as CEO of ME, Inc. will be different. As you implement your Strategic Life Plan, you will use your long-range vision to guide you through each day, week, month, quarter and year. You will connect your day-to-day appointments and daily to do list with your mission. In that way, rather than being distractions that keep you from reaching your goals, your daily activities become stepping stones to achieving them.

In Chapter 4, you completed a series of activities that helped you to break down your goals into daily tasks. Those tasks, completed one day at a time, will help you to implement your core strategies and carry out your long-term vision.

There is an old saying that I love. "How do you eat an elephant? One bite at a time." Action steps break your plan down into bite-sized pieces. For example, I love rainbow sherbet. I might eat a 30-pound tub of sherbet over a three-year period; however, I'm not going to eat it all in a day, regardless of how much I enjoy it. It's simply not feasible. I'm puzzled, then, as to why people would expect success when they attempt to accomplish a three-year goal in the last few weeks before the deadline instead of working towards the goal incrementally during the three years as intended. In order to reach your long-term goals, you must break them down into short-term and immediate goals and begin acting upon them right away.

If you set a three-year goal and delay working on it, it becomes less and less likely that you will reach it with each passing day. If you set a three-year goal today and get started today, you will actually have 1,095 days to reach your goal.

So how do you master your day so that your long-term goals don't get lost in the chaos of other daily duties? I have three suggestions.

1. **Keep a Prioritized Daily To Do List** – You learned how to create a prioritized to do list in the last chapter. This list is crucial because it allows you link your daily tasks to your weekly goals and monthly milestones which, in turn, connect to your quarterly targets and annual goals. Don't forget to identify your "Today Goal" – your most important task for the day. If possible, complete your most critical tasks first before moving on to the others. Mark your tasks completed when they are done. This will give you a sense of accomplishment and increase your productivity. In addition, use your to do list as a compass. If you are pulled away from the items on your list by a crisis or sidetracked by some other activity, always regroup by revisiting your to do list before moving on to the next task. This will help you to refocus on what is important to you.

2. **Open and Close Each Day with Planning** – Take about 15 minutes at the beginning and end of your day to plan. Start your day by updating your to do list and reviewing your schedule for the day. Close out your day by reviewing your to do list and getting yourself organized for the next day. You will be surprised how much difference a half an hour makes! Opening and closing your day with planning offers the structure you need to keep yourself focused on your long-term goals and priorities.

3. **Act Like the CEO** – We've already established that you are the Chief Executive Officer of ME, Inc. Now act like it every day. I have adopted the following acronym for CEO that I read and internalize during my planning time each morning.

CHAPTER FIVE

C: Cultivate – to cultivate means to develop or prepare for growth. Today, I commit to learn, grow and get better in every facet of my life. I will cultivate an attitude of gratitude and responsibility rather than complaining and blaming. I will embrace life-long learning and end the day as a wiser, better person.

E: Execute – to execute means to carry out or produce. Today, I commit to act upon my values, goals and priorities to produce results that will benefit me and others. I will carry out my duties with confidence and excellence and be a good steward of the resources entrusted to my care. I will make tangible progress towards my long-term goals.

O: Overcome – to overcome means to succeed when dealing with a problem or a difficulty. Today, I will courageously confront every challenge that I encounter. The stumbling blocks that I face today will become stepping stones tomorrow. I will problem solve and find an opportunity in every obstacle.

Take the Challenge

I know that you are committed to changing your life or you would not have made it this far in the book. Commitment is a critical and necessary component of your success; however, commitment in and of itself is not enough. You must have discipline. For example, you may be committed to losing ten pounds and lack the discipline to do what's necessary to achieve the goal and maintain the weight. Without discipline, your Strategic Life Plan will have all the teeth of a typical New Year's resolution.

There is one additional task that we must tackle as we cascade your mission and vision down to your daily routine so that you can develop the discipline to "Do It!" The way you discipline yourself in regards to your habits—your day-to-day behavior patterns—helps to determine your level of success. Think about it. Each day, your habits shape your choices and decisions. Each of us has good habits (those which are desirable and help to propel us forward), as well as bad habits (those which deter us and prevent us from maximizing our potential). Good habits help to keep you focused and moving toward your goals; bad habits distract you and move you farther away from hitting your target.

Athletes know how important it is to practice and form good habits when it comes to physical training. They persistently push past pain and discomfort to condition and prepare their bodies for winning the competition. Much less frequently, however, do we find people who are willing to apply this theory to change their mental habits.

www.trailblazers-inc.com

Mental habits are basically formed and broken in the same way as physical ones—through consistent daily practice. Much like developing or breaking physical habits, taking on mental habits requires patience, fortitude and diligence. Yet, it is worth it.

For years, I conducted annual retreats for women during the week between Christmas and New Year's Day. We would hideaway in log cabins in Rhode Island for a special time of reflection about the year that was closing and plan for the year that lay ahead. Those retreats provided much insight for me on how to turn wishes into real, tangible goals that are achieved.

One of the activities that we started during the later years was the 30-Day Challenge. In an effort to keep up the momentum that began at the retreat, every woman made a pledge that she would tackle a challenging area over the next month and develop a new habit to try to counter the old one that held her back. We saw tremendous success! Your final task in this chapter is to choose a habit that you would like to develop or break over the next 30 days.

30-Day Challenge Exercise Part 1: Habits to Break and Habits to Make

The first step is to brainstorm a list of habits you want to develop or break. In the table that follows, brainstorm a list of habits that you need to develop and a list of habits that you need to break in order to achieve your goals and live out the theme that you have selected for the upcoming year.

If you prefer, visit our website at *www.trailblazers-inc.com* and download the list of habits worksheet there.

Liberty's List of Habits

Habits to Break	Habits to Make
Snacking when under stress	Drinking water
Lateness	Arriving on time
Negative self-talk	Reciting Positive Affirmations
Avoiding conflict by shutting down	Asserting myself during conflict

My List of Habits

Habits to Break	Habits to Make

Narrowing the Field

While all of the habits on your list are worth addressing, it is extremely important to narrow your focus and concentrate on one habit at a time. If you attend to more than one habit at a time, you're setting yourself up for failure. Keep it simple and allow yourself to focus, so that you can give yourself the best chance for success. Choosing the right habit to tackle first is important. By experiencing success in breaking or making your first habit, you create momentum for addressing additional habits in the future and for other areas of your life to be influenced in a positive manner.

ACTIVITY

30-Day Challenge Exercise
Part 2: Pay Off Matrix

The Pay Off Matrix that follows will help you to select the initial habit to focus upon. It measures two important factors for each habit. The first is significance. Begin with the habit at the top of your list. Ask yourself: "If I develop or break this habit over the next month, how much closer would it bring me to achieving my goals and living my theme for this year? How important is this habit to helping me achieve success and fulfillment in other areas? How big of a win would it be for me to break or make this habit?" Decide whether the habit is of low, medium or high significance.

Next, consider the difficulty involved in making/breaking this particular habit. 30 days is a good number to get you started; however, the truth is that some habits are more difficult to break than others. The time it takes to replace an old habit is inconclusive because it depends entirely on the person and how long they have "owned" the habit to begin with. Think of a habit as a tree. A habit that is fairly new is like a young sapling with short roots that you can pull straight from the ground. A habit that you have owned for many years is like an old oak tree that has long roots that extend far underground. New smokers can break their habits fairly quickly. People who have smoked for most of their lives know how difficult it is to break that habit. Decide whether the habit is of low, medium or high difficulty. Plot the habit on the Pay Off Matrix according to its significance and difficulty.

CHAPTER FIVE

Liberty's Payoff Matrix

	LOW	MEDIUM	HIGH
HIGH	Recite and listen to affirmation CDs at bedtime **A**	Break habit of lateness/Develop punctuality. **B**	Pray daily **C**
MEDIUM	Read a book per month **D**	Walk laps **E**	Drink (4) 16 oz. bottles of water daily **F**
LOW	Stop leaving dishes in sink overnight/Do dishes nightly **G**	Stop allowing laundry to pile up/Wash clothes weekly **H**	Stop snacking when under pressure/Replace junk food with fresh fruit **I**

SIGNIFICANCE

DIFFICULTY

My Payoff Matrix

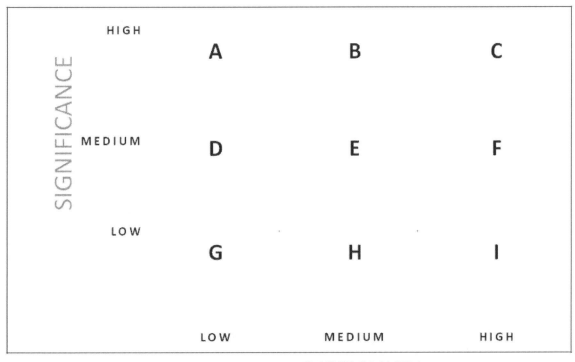

Finding a Gem

I suggest that you begin with a habit that is high in significance and low in difficulty. This will set you up for an easy win. Habits that are A's on the Pay Off Matrix are gems. They are considered "low hanging fruit" because they are easy to do and offer a big payoff. B's offer a high payoff, as well, but they are a bit more difficult to tackle. D's are easy to tackle, but do not have as high a payoff as A's. E's are middle of the road when it comes to pay off and of medium level significance. When possible, choose a habit that ranks as an A, B, D or E (in order of preference) for your first 30-day challenge. As you successfully kick or form a habit, you can move on and choose a new habit to focus upon.

CHAPTER FIVE

30-Day Challenge Exercise
Part 3: Habit to Address

Write the habit that you will focus upon in the space provided.

Habit Liberty Will Focus On:

> *I will target the habit of lying awake at night meditating on worse case scenarios by making a new habit of listening to positive affirmation CDs at bedtime.*

Habit I Will Focus On:

30-Day Challenge Exercise
Part 4: Identify Your Motivation

You need to be clear on why you are targeting the habit that you have chosen. The benefits of doing it need to be apparent. What reasons do you have for changing in this area? What benefits will you gain? Write down three strong reasons why you want to target this habit.

Liberty's Motivation:

1. *Targeting this habit will help me to rest better and stop having nightmares.*

2. *Targeting this habit will help me to become a more positive thinker.*

3. *Targeting this habit will help me to reach my goals by boosting my self-confidence.*

My Motivation:

30-Day Challenge Exercise
Part 5: Identify Potential Barriers and Distractions

Write down every potential obstacle that you can think of that may block you from forming or overcoming your target habit. If you are trying to break a habit, write down potential triggers. For each obstacle or trigger that you identify, come up with one or two ways to counter, avoid or prevent them.

Liberty's Obstacles/Triggers

Obstacles/Triggers	Ways to Overcome/Counter Them
Negative thoughts during sleep which lead to bad dreams	*Record affirmations onto a CD and play them as I fall asleep.*
Absentmindedness in forgetting to listen to affirmation CDs	*Keep the CD in the CD player in my bedroom. Create a decorative reminder card and place it on my night stand so that I will see it each night as I set the alarm.*
Negative self-talk	*Identify negative thoughts as they arise and immediately replace them with positive affirmation in that area.*

My Obstacles/Triggers

Obstacles/Triggers	Ways to Overcome/Counter Them

30-Day Challenge Exercise
Part 6: Get Support

Who will you turn to when you need encouragement? Who will hold you accountable? Get your family and friends and co-workers to support you. Ask them for their help, and let them know how important this is. You may even want to consider finding a buddy who wants to undertake the challenge with you. Write down the names of those who will support you in your endeavor to complete the 30-Day Challenge.

Liberty's Support System

My fiancé, Carl

My Support System

30-Day Challenge Exercise
Part 7: Stay Positive and Persist

You talk to yourself, in your head, all the time — but often you're not consciously aware of these thoughts. Start listening. These thoughts can derail any habit change or goal. Often they're negative: "I can't do this. This is too difficult. Why am I putting myself through this?" You will have negative thoughts — the important thing is to realize when you're having them, and push them out of your head. Eliminate negative self-talk and replace it with positive thoughts like, "I can do this!" Consider developing daily affirmations to encourage yourself. Be your own cheerleader. Give yourself pep talks. In the space provided, write an affirmation that you can use to cheer yourself on during the 30-Day Challenge.

CHAPTER FIVE

Liberty's Affirmations

I think positive, healthy thoughts.
I sleep soundly and rest well.
I am fearless and as bold as a lion.

My Affirmations

ACTIVITY 30-Day Challenge Exercise Part 8: Move on to a New Habit

Once you have successfully tackled one habit, return to your list of "habits to break" and "habits to make" and select a new habit to confront.

In the appendix, you will find additional worksheets to assist you with the 30-Day Challenge. The first is a 30-Day Challenge Record. Use this worksheet to keep track of your daily progress. The second worksheet is a 30-Day Challenge Pledge. Read and sign it, then keep it somewhere that you can see it to remind yourself of your commitment.

Kicking off your 30-Day Challenge is the last piece of the puzzle. You are now ready to launch Me, Inc., so let's "Do It!" – TODAY!

Countdown to Launch

Chart your progress by shading in the
steps that you have completed.

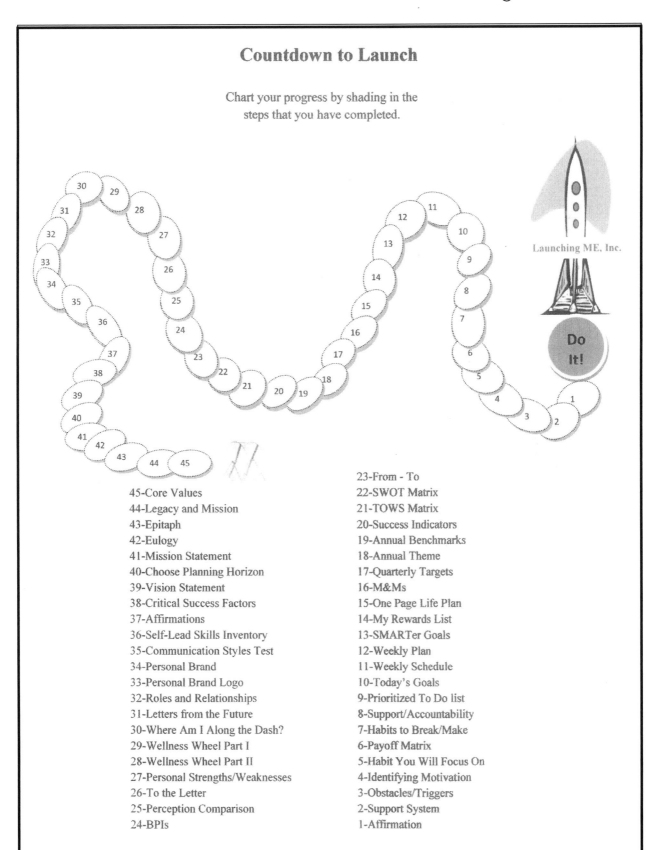

Launching ME, Inc.

Do It!

45-Core Values	23-From - To
44-Legacy and Mission	22-SWOT Matrix
43-Epitaph	21-TOWS Matrix
42-Eulogy	20-Success Indicators
41-Mission Statement	19-Annual Benchmarks
40-Choose Planning Horizon	18-Annual Theme
39-Vision Statement	17-Quarterly Targets
38-Critical Success Factors	16-M&Ms
37-Affirmations	15-One Page Life Plan
36-Self-Lead Skills Inventory	14-My Rewards List
35-Communication Styles Test	13-SMARTer Goals
34-Personal Brand	12-Weekly Plan
33-Personal Brand Logo	11-Weekly Schedule
32-Roles and Relationships	10-Today's Goals
31-Letters from the Future	9-Prioritized To Do list
30-Where Am I Along the Dash?	8-Support/Accountability
29-Wellness Wheel Part I	7-Habits to Break/Make
28-Wellness Wheel Part II	6-Payoff Matrix
27-Personal Strengths/Weaknesses	5-Habit You Will Focus On
26-To the Letter	4-Identifying Motivation
25-Perception Comparison	3-Obstacles/Triggers
24-BPIs	2-Support System
	1-Affirmation

The Conclusion: It's Time to Cut the Ribbon

In just a few months, my son will graduate from high school. Dressed in his regalia, he will march down the aisle during the school's commencement ceremony to receive his diploma.

I have always loved the term "commencement" for, although the ceremony marks the end of high school, commencement means beginning or the time at which something actually starts. I'm so excited for my son!! An entirely new world is about to open up to him. And, so it is with you.

Although the last chapter brought this workbook to an end, you are standing on the verge of a brand new beginning. You are poised for a launch!

Launch ('länch):

To enter enthusiastically into something; to plunge

To send forth, catapult, or release

To begin a new venture or phase; to embark

To set in motion

Consider holding a ribbon cutting ceremony. Gather your dearest friends and family and let them know you've been promoted to CEO and wanted to celebrate the launch of your new company—ME, Inc. You are about to enthusiastically enter into something great; your rocket ship is on the launching pad and you are about to embark on a wonderful journey. Are you ready? Go ahead and push the launch button. You're the CEO...you've been empowered to set it all in motion!

www.trailblazers-inc.com

Appendix

Daily Record Worksheet
30-Day Challenge

Date:	**Date:**	**Date:**
Affirmations: □ yes □ no	**Affirmations:** □ yes □ no	**Affirmations:** □ yes □ no
Today's Progress:	**Today's Progress:**	**Today's Progress:**
Date:	**Date:**	**Date:**
Affirmations: □ yes □ no	**Affirmations:** □ yes □ no	**Affirmations:** □ yes □ no
Today's Progress:	**Today's Progress:**	**Today's Progress:**
Date:	**Date:**	**Date:**
Affirmations: □ yes □ no	**Affirmations:** □ yes □ no	**Affirmations:** □ yes □ no
Today's Progress:	**Today's Progress:**	**Today's Progress:**
Date:	**Date:**	**Date:**
Affirmations: □ yes □ no	**Affirmations:** □ yes □ no	**Affirmations:** □ yes □ no
Today's Progress:	**Today's Progress:**	**Today's Progress:**
Date:	**Date:**	**Date:**
Affirmations: □ yes □ no	**Affirmations:** □ yes □ no	**Affirmations:** □ yes □ no
Today's Progress:	**Today's Progress:**	**Today's Progress:**
Date:	**Date:**	**Date:**
Affirmations: □ yes □ no	**Affirmations:** □ yes □ no	**Affirmations:** □ yes □ no
Today's Progress:	**Today's Progress:**	**Today's Progress:**
Date:	**Date:**	**Date:**
Affirmations: □ yes □ no	**Affirmations:** □ yes □ no	**Affirmations:** □ yes □ no
Today's Progress:	**Today's Progress:**	**Today's Progress:**
Date:	**Date:**	**Date:**
Affirmations: □ yes □ no	**Affirmations:** □ yes □ no	**Affirmations:** □ yes □ no
Today's Progress:	**Today's Progress:**	**Today's Progress:**
Date:	**Date:**	**Date:**
Affirmations: □ yes □ no	**Affirmations:** □ yes □ no	**Affirmations:** □ yes □ no
Today's Progress:	**Today's Progress:**	**Today's Progress:**
Date:	**Date:**	**Date:**
Affirmations: □ yes □ no	**Affirmations:** □ yes □ no	**Affirmations:** □ yes □ no
Today's Progress:	**Today's Progress:**	**Today's Progress:**

Pledge Worksheet
30-Day Challenge

I, _____, commit to the following for the next 30 days:

· I will practice daily the behavior(s) that will lead to the development or elimination of the habit that I am targeting.

· I will use daily affirmations to keep me motivated and on track.

· I will use the techniques that I have developed to eliminate barriers or distractions when I encounter them.

· I will review my plan and progress with my partner on at least a weekly basis.

· I will record my progress on a daily basis.

· I will remain attentive and watchful for lessons learned that I can apply in the future.

Signature_____

Date _____

MANAGING DETOURS

List everything about this situation that is important to you right now. Prioritize your list.

- ○
- ○
- ○
- ○
- ○
- ○
- ○
- ○
- ○

Think about your circle of control. Make a decision not to focus your energy on things you cannot change. Ask yourself instead, "What can I do to influence the situation positively and bring about a change?" Write your response in the space provided, then integrate your new goals into your Strategic Life Plan.

Number	To-Do	By When